HIMPOSSIBLE

Adventures in Faith

Stan Gain

Visit Holy Fire Publishing at www.holyfirepublishing.com

ISBN: 978-1-60383-600-5

Published by:
Holy Fire Publishing
www.HolyFirePublishing.com

Cover Design: Jay Cookingham

Printed in the United States of America, The United Kingdom and Australia

Table of Contents

Introduction

For many years people have been saying to me, *"Stan, you really should write a book about your experiences!"* For just as many years I resisted. To write a biographical account seemed to me somewhat boastful. If you read further into this book you will see that in terms of who I am, I am no one special. Even that to me sounds like false humility! I did not come from a noble or rich family. I neither studied well at school nor achieved great academic success. Yet I have seen God at work in so many circumstances as I have travelled the world.

I will take you to a simple meeting in a humble rural church in India to a confrontation with the KGB in USSR as it was called at that time. I will take you from countless 'crusade meetings' around the world to the heart-breaking sadness of slavery in the brick kilns of Pakistan. I will take you from stories of salvation to accounts of deliverance. And so much more! Whilst the book for obvious reasons centres around me I have endeavoured to ensure that any and all glory goes to God. I have nothing to boast about.

Without Him none of the things that follow would have been possible. The direction my life before He took hold of me and I took hold of Him was most definitely on a downward spiral. I would have had so very little to write about prior to 10th August 1982. I hope this book is an encouragement to you to experience the life-changing power of God when He comes to infill us with His Holy Spirit. It can be summed up in the words of one of my favourite songs: -

> *Father God, I wonder how I managed to exist Without the knowledge of Your parenthood and Your loving care. But now I am Your son, I am adopted in Your family And I can never be alone 'Cause Father God, You're here beside me*   (Ian Smale)

I do not keep statistics, nor do I have a diary of all that has happened. I did on my earlier travels in Africa keep a short diary but over the years this has been mislaid. All that I have written has come from a rich store of experiences and memories. What I know is that I have been privileged to travel to and through over 70 nations as I have bought the good news of Jesus Christ to many millions. I have preached over the radio to more than 2 million people in Spanish speaking South America and have spoken under an avocado tree in Kenya where myself, my driver and my interpreter doubled the size of the congregation. I am neither impressed by large congregations nor disappointed by very humble ones. Whenever I have the opportunity to speak of my beloved Jesus, I do so with enthusiasm.

If you will permit me to boast a little and whet your appetite for those things that I have included in the following pages, I trust you will not consider me prideful. It is more as an example of what can be achieved if one chooses to firstly, walk closely with the Living God and secondly, believe that all the promises that are found in His Word, the Bible, are true. Having taken far from perfect steps within these two parameters, I have experienced two local revivals, one in the UK and one in Africa. I have seen, probably, more than ten thousand men, women and children responding to the Gospel call for salvation. I am sure I have heard more than a thousand testimonies of supernatural healing. I have seen scores of miracles. I have written four books, this being the third that is published. I have written a training course for new Christians and rural pastors. I have stood for election in our Parliament on three occasions (thankfully unsuccessfully!) I could not count the number of times I must have circumnavigated the earth… There we are! That is the end of my *boasting*. I hope you will forgive me, but I hope it will draw you into the following pages.

My main purpose in writing is not primarily to tell my story but to encourage you, dear reader, to understand that if you are willing, God can use you too. Your calling may not be the same as mine, but to the willing and open heart with a simple trust in Him, I guarantee He will use you in a greater way then He may have done at any time up to this point in your life.

There is often a lot of cynicism when talking or recounting supernatural events. We live in an empirical world where we have been taught that everything must be established by fact or by science. Faith transcends these things. It does not mean that we blindly follow but we simply believe. I must ask you to simply accept that everything I have written I have seen and experienced. If not, you must consider me a liar and a fraud!

To help in understanding, I have found the following two quotations about miracles to be very helpful in explaining the supernatural lifestyle that Christianity presents. The first is from G K Chesterton who wrote:-

If a man believes in unalterable natural law, he cannot believe in any miracle in any age. If a man believes in a will behind law, he can believe in any miracle in any age.

A W Tozer wrote:-

God does not sell himself into the hands of religious magicians. I do not believe in that kind of miracle. I believe in the kind of miracles that God gives to his people who live so close to him that answers to prayer are common and these miracles are not uncommon.

Enough introduction. It is time to introduce you to my 'Adventures in Faith' where everything is HIMpossible.

Chapter 1

A Sunbeam

So how did a fairly normal, fairly average man end up sitting under a tree in a brick kiln in Pakistan face to face with a member of the Taliban armed with an AK-47 and being told that the price for the release of a slave family would be one bullet!

Let me take you on a journey of faith from my own experiences as I have walked It, based on the truth of God's promise that *'if we believe, nothing shall be impossible to us'*.

In fact, everything is **HIMpossible!**

For several years people have been suggesting that I should write an autobiography. I have been reluctant because I have not particularly wanted to write about myself. As a consequence I have tried to write about an adventure of faith in the hope that the Lord Jesus will shine through over and above myself. Having said that this first chapter is about my earlier years as I considered it necessary to set a context for the main theme of this book. I think it is fair to say that there has never been a time in my life when I have not understood that Jesus died on the cross as a sacrifice for our sins. I have never doubted his supernatural virgin birth nor his bodily resurrection on that first Easter Sunday. Consequently, in the years covered by this first chapter I would never have denied my faith, but my understanding was very much a mental assent rather than a faith-filled discipleship.

I was born in 1947, the third of four children, having two older sisters Janet and Vivien. My younger brother, Peter, was to be born many years after me in 1963. This was a true age of austerity following the end of the Second World War. We lived together on the fifth floor in a flat on a council estate in Charlton, south-east London. I can say confidently that we were a happy family and that our childhoods were similarly happy, although like any family with small children, we had our moments! We were certainly not a rich family in material terms, but neither were any of the families in our world. There was much love and security as we grew up together. My father worked at the local gas company and my mother stayed at home working hard to raise three children in these difficult days. Not that we went without, but I am convinced that our parents often went without for us, although I could never get them to admit this.

We were what some have called a part of the 'Sunday School generation'. Those born between the mid-1940s and 1950s whose parents, probably wanting some peace and quiet, sent their children to Sunday School. I loved Sunday School. There were dozens of children from the local council estates but not so many from church families as is the case these days. I loved singing such songs as *"Jesus wants me for a Sunbeam!"* Whether he finally got a Sunbeam I will leave it for the reader to decide! So many of the songs that we sung were simply verses from the Bible. Another favourite song in those days, which I learned to love as I grew older, was based on John 14, *'I am the way, the truth and the life. No one comes to the Father but through me.'*

On 1st September 1952, my fifth birthday, I started my education and I loved it - for two days. I can remember on the third day not wanting to go back to Charlton Manor School again, I have a vivid memory of me sitting on Miss Lowe's lap crying my eyes out wanting to go back home. After all, I had had two days of school and was ready for a new adventure! However, I soon settled in and really enjoyed my days in both the infant and junior schools. At this age, I devoured the learning, so much so, that I jumped a year and was put into a class a year ahead of my age-mates and I even came second in a class of 48 children at the end of my final year of junior school.

The transition between junior school and secondary education seemed to mark a change of direction. Following success at the 11+ examination

I found myself a pupil at what was then called Roan Grammar School for Boys. It was a good academic school but I never really settled in. My experience there was so vastly different from that of my primary education. I have never been tall in stature and as the youngest and probably the smallest in the school I was sometimes the victim of mild bullying. To overcome this I found the best solution was to make friends with the more mischievous boys and it was not an uncommon thing to find myself outside the headmaster's office to explain my behaviour and receive yet another detention.

Whilst I do not doubt that the school had a good academic record it was not the best school for me. I was, as the expression goes, 'bored out of my skull' and did not really take my studies seriously. I can remember many times sitting through a lesson looking wistfully out of the window without giving much attention to the teacher. I have subsequently learned that the best form of teaching is not to impart knowledge but rather to inspire pupils to want to learn for themselves. Sadly, on reflection, it seemed to me that the impartation of knowledge was their method. When my mother recently passed away I found that she had kept all my school reports. On almost all of them the headmaster had written comments suggesting that I could have achieved much better results if I had applied myself. As I grew older I applied myself less and less and eventually found that the pleasures of Greenwich Park were far greater than those of school. I created many devious ways to miss lessons and to my dubious credit was never discovered. Somehow I managed to leave school with enough education and certificates to satisfy future employers.

My contact with the church has been a constant factor throughout my life. At the age of seven I joined the Life Boys which was then known as the Junior Reserve of the Boys Brigade. As with most things outside of school I threw myself into the activities that were offered. At the same time as starting secondary school I transferred to the 2nd West Kent (Blackheath) Company. I am eternally grateful to the Boys Brigade as I believe it kept me on the straight and narrow and tempered my rebellious nature. At the time of my joining there were exactly 100 boys in the company section drawn mainly from the council housing estates in the area. I made many good friends at that time and I am still in touch with a fair few of them today. In the winter months there was a full programme of activities including gymnastics, brass and bugle bands, sports, badge work, drill and Bible Class. Much more interesting than the academic studies of school. I was at the hall every night of the week and Bible Class on a Sunday morning. There was a competition for perfect attendance at every drill night and every Bible Class which meant we had to be 'never absent and never late' for these two activities from September to May. I achieved five 'perfect attendances' and missed only one drill night in six years because of sickness. As a result, even today, I hate being late for anything and will turn up ridiculously early rather than be late for an appointment.

One of the strengths of the 2nd West Kent was the drill. The London District held an annual drill competition, the final of which was competed for at the famous Royal Albert Hall in London. It was a credit to the drill officer that boys from the local council estates were moulded into a fine drill company. For the six years I was in the company section, we appeared in the final every year. For four years we were the winners. I count it as the highlight of my Boys Brigade life that as senior NCO in my final year I had the honour of collecting the Daily Telegraph shield in that prestigious venue on behalf of the winning company.

Living as we did on a council estate it was not difficult for me to become involved in much of the mischief that young teenage boys tend to find. With the self-preservation methods I had learned at secondary school it was not long that through peer pressure I started smoking at the age of 13. This quickly developed into a serious addiction. I was also persuaded at the age of about 15 to enter the Royal Oak public house for my first pint of mild shandy! Although these activities may not seem particularly unusual, they both led to more serious problems later in life. If there was mischief to be found I was often in the thick of it with those who were the chief mischief makers. We often played a game called 'knock down ginger'. Traditionally, this was simply knocking at someone's front door and running away before they could answer. We developed a more sophisticated version involving a milk bottle, cotton and one of the lifts in the blocks of flats in which we lived. When we found a loose door knocker we would tie the cotton around the milk bottle and through the knocker. We would then go down in the lift and at a certain distance would break the cotton. This caused the door to knock and the milk bottle to break on the doorstep, but we would be far away!

Not that my life was all mischief. We would often go down to the River Thames and find pieces of chalk which could be used for playing tracking games. Although we did not fully appreciate the significance of the bomb sites, we did find them a valuable source of pram wheels and we had great fun building box carts. I still have a couple of scars on my body from accidents but it was never anything too serious. These were the days before 'Health and Safety' and it was nothing for our mum to pack us off for day with a mini picnic and so long as she knew where we were, there was no immediate danger.

At this time of my life it would be fair to say that I lived at two levels. On the one level was the mischief maker and on the other, a regular church attender. As I have said, I have always been attached to the church. At the age of 15 I was confirmed in the Church of England. Whilst I was very sincere in my commitment I was never really discipled in Christian living. I can remember the vicar telling me during the confirmation classes, *"Do not expect anything to happen when the Bishop lays his hands upon you!"* He was certainly a man of faith as absolutely nothing happened! Whether I was not properly discipled or whether I did not take the Bible Class lessons seriously I do not know.

In my final years at school I discovered a way of being in school for registration but absent from the lessons. I am not sure whether it is creditable, but I was never caught. Some afternoons when I should have been at school I was earning money. I even developed my own mini business cutting the lawns of elderly people. This apart, I always managed to find small errands and part-time jobs to earn money - mainly to buy cigarettes! These jobs were many and varied, ranging from helping the baker and milkman on their rounds to working in a service station and even cooking doughnuts in a confectioners. I had a weekend job with a local garage and learnt how to service and maintain cars.

On the Easter holidays before I finally left school I took a job with the Inland Revenue at Somerset House. I was offered a full-time job with them and started in a tax office at the Elephant and Castle. I had some fairly notorious villains in my caseload. Surprisingly, I was financially worse off when I started work as I was now responsible for contributing towards my upkeep, buying my own clothes, paying taxes and travelling expenses. I enjoyed work very much and was soon able to buy my first car. It was a 1954 Ford Popular for which I paid the grand sum of £16. (Such was my financial state that I paid for it in three instalments.) I remember the insurance for the first year was £29.

When I bought the car I could not drive but with the help of a friend spent two evenings learning. Unlike modern cars it lacked synchromesh and only had three gears and a top speed of 54 mph. Three days after taking delivery of the car we set out on a 300-mile journey to St Ives in Cornwall and a pony trekking holiday! It took about 20 hours to get there but we arrived incident free. In that week I drove some 800 miles and after only six lessons was able to pass my driving test at the first attempt. Thinking back, I guess I have always had the temperament to say, "*Yes I can,*" rather than "*No I can't.*" For example, I signed a form to say that I could swim 50 yards fully clothed, when I could not swim a stroke so I could spend a weekend canoeing on the River Wye.

I enjoyed the work with the Inland Revenue. It was varied and I met many people. In the evenings, to supplement my income and enable me to afford my bad habits, I took a part-time job as a barman in the Bugle Horn pub in Charlton Village. This bar work did nothing to curb the addiction to nicotine and it strengthened what was fast becoming an addiction to alcohol. When my parents moved to Sheringham in

Norfolk I could not resist moving with them as they were buying a beautiful house with six bedrooms close to the sea: an amazing contrast to living on the fifth floor of a suburban council flat.

I found work in the taxation department of Norwich Union and travelled about 50 miles a day to and from work. Sadly, the quality of my cars did not improve. One such car cost me just £5 that someone won in a raffle but did not want. I took a part-time job in the Red Lion in Upper Sheringham and the landlord often offset my wages by keeping my cars roadworthy. I later worked as office manager for Standard Life. Having lived in London, North Norfolk was far too quiet, and I subsequently moved to Norwich. Again, now living on my own and responsible for all expenses, I supplemented my income working as barman at the Norfolk and Norwich Masonic Association. I learned from the inside about Freemasonry and am thankful that I was never inveigled into membership.

After a couple of years even Norwich proved too quiet and following a disappointing relationship that I had hoped would end in marriage, I returned to London and picked up from where I left off. I had several jobs, initially working for my brother-in-law in his new company Jason Transport. I eventually found myself delivering bathrooms and kitchens for an up and coming plumbers merchants - C P Hart. The brothers John and Tom were probably the best employers one could ask for. As an example, when I transferred to the accounts department, instead of providing me with a company car they gave me a company caravanette because of my work and camping activities at that time with the Boys Brigade. I had picked up again with the Boys Brigade on my return to London.

All through this time my craving for cigarettes and alcohol increased and so did my involvement with the church and the Boys Brigade. It seems strange looking back. How could these two things work side-by-side. It was as if on one side I was seeking after God but on the other remained content with the things of the world and the status quo. I knew the stories of the Bible and even taught them on a regular basis but as somebody said to me subsequently it is one thing to know the book but as Christians we need to know the author! This compartmentalisation of my life did not satisfy and did not truly work. In later life a friend, to my shame, said to me, *"I considered Christianity for myself, but when I looked at your life and others like you, I saw no real difference in the way you lived and decided that Christianity was not true!"* I still see this friend on a regular basis and to this day he has not been able to grasp the truth of Christianity.

For many years I continued walking these two paths. On the social side I was always the first to party. In fact, when sharing a flat with others we held some very 'successful' parties. The Boys Brigade had a very lively Old Boys Association and I enjoyed the social side very much, even one year being voted the 'clubman of the year.' On the church side I was not only a regular attender but served on the PCC of two local churches. I did not realise how divided my life had become until one evening at a PCC meeting that was going to go on beyond pub closing time I saw my hand begin to shake. I would not make it for a drink before they closed! This behaviour continued for some years and my unhappiness although known to me was not noticed by others. Maybe the deceit I had learned when 'hopping off' from school was not forgotten. My smoking habit had increased to almost 50 cigarettes a day and I frequented many different pubs so that I would not be known as a regular drinker in any of them. Neither of these things brought satisfaction and naturally had a very profound effect on my finances.

I am now a firm believer in the power of prayer, and I believe there were many people praying for me. I was at a Boys Brigade camp and I was in the position of Quartermaster. This responsibility was to ensure that there were sufficient supplies for the cook house and that all equipment was fit for purpose. I was sharing my 'company caravanette' with another member of staff. At night we often found ourselves in discussion about Christian things. On the Thursday it was my turn to speak at the morning service and I shared the story of Nicodemus. (John 3). Nicodemus was a leading member of the Jewish Council and came

11

to Jesus at night wanting a comfortable talk about religion. Jesus knowing his heart simply said to him, "*Nicodemus, you must be born again!*" This sparked a question from my friend, "*When did you become a Christian?*" I gave him what was at the time my standard answer that I had always been a Christian. I thought no more about it until the following week. On the Monday evening I was alone, having had several drinks on the way home. His question, "*When did you become a Christian?*" was gnawing away at me. I remembered a friend, Alan, who I knew had found God and decided to phone him and talk with him. It was a long conversation and he was preparing a Bible study for his own church on the love of God. He shared much of this with me and a part of his study was the story of Nicodemus!

I was at home alone and after considering Alan's words and reflecting on my own life, I decided the time had come for me to be serious about the things of God. I got out of my chair and knelt. I can remember word for word the prayer that I made that evening. "*Lord, I have made a mess of my life. I want to be born again. I want you to take over.*" That was it. Just a simple prayer. At the time I had no idea how one simple prayer could change a life. I remember I sat back in my chair, had another cigarette (that is all that I knew to do!) and went to bed.

And what a change it was to be ......!

Chapter 2

The Adventures Begin

Something had most certainly changed! I woke early the next morning and I knew something powerful had happened to me as I slept. I was not to know that this was the first day of a new and exciting adventure of faith. It is hard to describe. I can only say I felt *alive* for the first time. It was about six o'clock; much earlier than I usually woke. Instead of the usual heavy, drowsy feeling that I always suffered first thing in the morning, I felt fully awake and fully alert. My routine up to then had been to reach for the cigarettes at the side of my bed and I was usually smoking long before my feet hit the ground, but that morning I did not touch them. I did not want one; I did not crave one. Me, the one who failed almost every Monday morning in giving up smoking. I can honestly say that from that day I have never smoked again. I did not realise it at the time, but my addictions to both the nicotine and alcohol had been broken. The Lord had changed my life completely, even as I slept. The Bible says, *"If anyone is in Jesus Christ, he is a new creation. The old has gone! The new has come!"* (1 Corinthians 5:17) My short prayer of asking the Lord to take over my life had been answered in a most emphatic and powerful way. It was not a psychological or emotional happening. Over my first 35 years of life I had often made similar 'response' prayers to God and had no expectation of such a powerful and supernatural reply from Him on this occasion. He had truly answered my prayer and I was *'a new creation'.*

It was good to be alive and the following morning at six o'clock I found myself in Greenwich Park. The best way I can describe it is that I saw the colours of the flowers, the beauty of the clouds and the music of the birdsong for the first time. Yes! Of course I had seen these things before but on that morning everything was elevated to a new level. I was walking as if on air! When God created Adam in the Garden of Eden, the Bible says that He Himself would come down in the cool of the evening and walk with Adam. It truly felt as if I were walking with God Himself in Greenwich Park that morning.

The Bible says in many places that a believer should repent and believe. With this new-found relationship with the Living God I most certainly believed. After such a powerful encounter I have never doubted that my salvation is secure. I have often heard people say that when they come to the Lord they breakdown in floods of tears in repentance. In fact, I have seen this happen on many occasions as I have preached from a crusade meeting. For a few days my joy was overflowing but there was an occasion that I believe completed my repentance. The following weekend I was due to go and meet my parents at my sister's home in Essex. When the time came to leave I just could not go. I felt so unworthy to share the good news of my new birth in Jesus, to carry His name, that I broke down in tears. I was so broken that I sobbed and sobbed for many hours before falling into a deep sleep. When I awoke the next morning, I felt that my conscience was clear and from that time I have had a wonderful walk with the Lord. Not without challenges and difficulties but wonderful nevertheless.

The first year of my new life was like a 'honeymoon'. My awareness of the presence of God was full. I was hungry to know more of Him - not just about him as my years of *'churchianity'* had taught me - but to know Him and build my relationship with Him. My Bible knowledge suddenly came to life and the stories that I had taught for so long became so real to me. It is difficult to explain. It was as if I had been elevated to a new reality. I was a regular visitor to the local Christian bookshop and would often buy several books on each visit. The first book I read, *'Through Gates of Splendour'* was particularly challenging as I read about the life of a missionary to Ecuador, Jim Elliott. He was totally sold out for God and eventually lost his life to the Auka Indians. One of his sayings was *"he is no fool who gives up what he cannot keep to gain what he cannot lose."* His biography also challenged me to spend at least one hour in prayer before my day started. This was the beginning of my prayer life. No longer repeating the liturgical prayers that I had learned but talking to my heavenly Father in real relationship and hearing clearly from Him.

I was no longer just a churchgoer but coveted every opportunity to worship the Lord and hear His word. Thankfully, I sat under the teaching of a very solid preacher and found his preaching both challenging and edifying. This was a church that practised baptism by full immersion and although I had been confirmed in the Church of England I now felt the need to be fully baptised. When the time came for me to give a testimony, I am told that I spoke for a full fifteen minutes! I was given several baptismal presents and cards. One was a book entitled *"Rees Howell - Intercessor."* By Norman Grubb. Apart from the Bible itself, this book had a profound and significant effect on my life. Rees Howell was a man who walked in total obedience to the Holy Spirit and I was challenged to follow his example. He eventually founded the Bible School of Wales, a true faith venture. Although no longer a Bible college, I recently visited and the man who was assistant to Rees's son laid hands on me and prayed over me – a deeply moving experience.

I really loved this church and the teaching but was disappointed that when Luis Palau planned to hold a large tent meeting on Blackheath the elders chose not to be part of it. In consequence, I reluctantly changed my attendance to St John's in Blackheath who were fully involved. I loved this mission and trained as a counsellor. I attended every night and took many people to hear the truth of the Gospel. It was a real joy to see hundreds of people responding to the call of the good news of Jesus night after night. The mission was extended for one month at QPR football ground in West London and most evenings I drove a battered minibus across London in the rush hour to take people to hear the preaching.

Although I had received no teaching concerning spiritual gifts (more about this in later chapters), it was during this mission that I received my first' *word of prophecy'.* One Saturday night a violent storm damaged the circus tent that was being used and the meeting was transferred to the local town hall. During the time of worship the Lord spoke to me with two Scriptures relevant to the situation. The first from Jeremiah 31:36 '*Restrain your voice from weeping and your eyes from tears, for your work will* be rewarded' and verse 21 'Set up road signs; put up guideposts. Take note of the highway, the road that you take'. I was not fully sure what they meant but felt compelled to deliver them by letter to the mission chairman next morning. Imagine my amazement and delight when driving past the tent that evening to see a huge sign at the side of the road simply stating, 'MEETING HERE TONIGHT'. Here was the 'road sign' on the highway, a major route in and out of London. I was even more delighted when the letter was read aloud, and anonymously, at the meeting as a confirmation of the accuracy of prophecy.

There were many signs of a mini revival in the area. There were 128 people in need of discipleship referred to St John's Church and at one time there were six classes for new Christians running concurrently. I was overjoyed to see so many coming into the Kingdom of God. I do not settle easily into the liturgical style of the Anglican church. I was often perturbed on a Sunday morning to see these new Christians, who were swelling the church congregation, struggling with hymn books, prayer books, service sheets and notice sheets. Having come from the open style of the tent mission they seemed confused by the language of the prayer book, especially when it was in the language of the 1662 Book of Common Prayer. I often spoke to the vicar about this, but my protests made little difference. I am not known for being the most patient of men, and one Friday in my exasperation at the thought of another '1662 service' I decided to act. Before the following Sunday service, which was to be from the Book of Common Prayer, I went into the church and hid all the prayer books in what was then a dusty unused gallery. I then phoned the vicar and told him that we would no longer be using these books in the morning service as the books were no longer available! We entered into a long discussion and although I agreed to return the prayer books, it was the last '1662 service' that the church held on a Sunday morning. I passionately believe that the church should be both relevant and understandable.

I was still involved with the Boys Brigade and this revival continued through the summer camp that year. Through that week of camp there was an almost tangible presence of God. One night, the Holy Spirit moved sovereignly through the camp. Evening tent prayers had finished and the staff were in the main marquee discussing the events of the day. One of the tent commanders came to the marquee with the report that one of the boys in his tent had become a Christian. It was not long before another boy came with the report that two boys in his tent had become Christians. That evening twelve boys gave their lives to Jesus. There had been no staff present in the tents. The Holy Spirit had moved quietly through the camp and brought salvation. Some people do not realise that revival is not always at national level but can be very localised. These mini revivals are just as valid as the sovereign move of God He can bring to nations.

Following on from the camp revival, a series of Bible studies began in the office of Mike, a local schoolteacher. These were invaluable in helping the new Christians, but people started to gossip and question what grown men were doing meeting with young boys on a regular basis! When they heard this, the boys started to pray that girls would join the group and the very next week a girl was introduced to the Bible studies. This spirit of revival continued through this group and it was not long before as many as 60 young people both boys and girls became part of what came to be known as the Thursday Group. It was wonderful to see the powerful prayer of this group. One week they would be praying for one of their friends to be saved and the next week they would turn up at the meeting and give their lives to the Lord.

In addition, it was a good introduction to learning about and practising spiritual gifts. I remember it was at this group that I first prayed for someone to be healed. I started simply with a young lady who had a headache. I prayed - nothing happened! I prayed again - still nothing happened! I was sure that the Bible was true and so prayed for a third time and this time she was healed. It was a first simple step into a ministry that in time would enable me to see many hundreds, maybe thousands, healed in the name of Jesus. The devil will often challenge the effectiveness of spiritual gifts. He challenged me that this young lady was not really healed but just said that she was to stop me praying! Many years later she confirmed to me that she remembered this incident and she was indeed healed. The Bible says that, *"The devil comes to kill and to steal and to destroy!"* *(John 10:10)* He was not able to steal on this occasion.

Around this time, I was still working full-time at the plumbers' supply company. The owners, John and Tom were fantastic employers but changes to the management structure also brought changes to the work environment. One particular day things were really tough. I had taken myself off to the sanctuary of the gents' toilet, my emergency prayer closet, and can remember asking the Lord to simply, *"Take me away from all this!"* Within about an hour one of the new managers called me into his office and told me that the many perks that I had been receiving were to be taken from me. I thanked him and resigned on the spot. He looked quite alarmed but for me it was the best day's work that he had ever done! Since that time, I have had no full-time work, although I have taken occasional part-time and temporary jobs to support my missionary travels. From this moment my dependency was no longer on a salary but was fully on the Lord!

When I left, I had about £320 in the bank and tried to work out a frugal budget. I could perhaps survive for three months since the rent I was paying was minimal. I refused to claim government assistance as I was learning dependency on God. Within a couple of weeks someone approached me with a severe financial crisis that could have cost him his home, his family and possibly his wife. I spent six pounds on a return coach trip to meet him. I asked him to write down exactly how much he needed to repay the debt and he handed me a piece of paper. Written on it was the sum of £312! That left me with just £2 and my frugal budget went out of the window! Now I was truly dependent on the Lord. I have many wonderful stories of how the Lord has provided, and I am sure many of them will crop up as I tell of this walk of faith! All I will say at this time is that in the more than thirty-five years that have since passed I have never been hungry, never been without a home, never been without transport, never been without clothes and have always had something to give when need has arisen.

To return to the young people, they were members of various local churches. At one time, the leaders prayed to see whether the Thursday Group should become a church. The consensus was that this was not the direction. Whilst praying, I felt the Lord moving me on from being a leader. St John's church was growing in number but somehow did not seem able to break through into the fullness of life that the Holy Spirit brings. Following a clear word from the Lord, the Charlton and Blackheath Christian Fellowship began on the 8th September 1985. Although my main calling at that time was as an evangelist I found myself becoming the pastor of this new church.

They were exciting days and during the meetings we were never certain how the Holy Spirit would turn up – but He always did! It was only three years since my 'conversion experience' and I was on a super-fast learning curve. I can remember during one mid-week Bible study one of the young people was suddenly thrown bodily against the wall still seated in his chair in a demonic manifestation. I had had no experience of this aspect of ministry at the time but as always, the Lord enabled me to deal with the situation. (Spiritual gifts - discernment of spirits). I learned to pray one of my shortest, yet most effective prayers… "H E L P!" When later revivals broke out in Toronto, Brownsville and other places I could never understand why people went to bring 'the revival' back to London when God was already at work in revival power. Revival does not dwell in a geographic environment but rather abides in the heart of those who honour and love God.

The church grew rapidly and being made up mainly of young people with little or no income I had no direct support from the church as the pastor for the first year. God provided in many miraculous ways. One day after the service I was clearing up the hall we were renting for our services and wedged between two chairs stacked at the side of the hall was an envelope bearing my name. I have no idea how it came to be there, and I could easily have missed it, but inside was over £300 which kept me going for quite some time. On another occasion, I went to visit a friend, a member of the band of the Parachute Regiment, who were playing in a local park. I had nothing in my pocket having just returned from Africa. There was much litter on the ground and I felt a prompting voice telling me to pick up a particularly dirty envelope. I do not make a habit of this but as I opened the envelope there was a crisp £50 note inside!

On another occasion I was walking to a friend's house across the local common. It had been raining and my feet were getting wet because of the holes in my shoes. After an enjoyable meal my host asked me about my shoe size. When I responded she said she had just bought a new pair of shoes for her son and they were the wrong size but were just my size. I walked back across the common that night with the dry feet and a brand-new pair of shoes! I was learning how God is faithful to his promises. I have mentioned that I sometimes took a temporary job to support ministry One such job was delivering parcels for a short period. As I was walking up the hill to my home, I heard the Lord say I want you to give up this job. I had a particularly heavy telephone bill of more than £100 as I had been supporting a young lady struggling in France with a youth mission. I reminded the Lord of this need and when I opened my front door there was a cheque with some £110 lying on the mat. Needless to say I left the job the following day!

After about three years the church had grown to close on a hundred people. Mission was a large part of the life of the fellowship. We often held open air meetings on the local council estates, and it was not unusual for the local residents to oppose us. I can remember two occasions being threatened with a knife and once, on a beautiful hot and sunny day, we were all refreshed when a bucket of water was thrown over us by an angry resident! In the autumn that year we held a week of mission at a local school that we called 'Break Free with Jesus'. Every night we had a different activity and we were amazed when Gloria Gaynor (Yes – that Gloria Gaynor of 'I Will Survive' fame) agreed to host an evening of song and testimony at a local community hall. She was launching into a new Christian era in her own career. It was probably the smallest audience that she had ever performed to and it was certainly the smallest donation she had ever received!

One thing I have always enjoyed is writing and would often compose small poems and lyrics for worship songs. I would not consider myself to be creatively musical - my attempt to play the cello in the school orchestra and the cornet in the Boys Brigade brass band bore little fruit. I was encouraged by a friend Mark, to write lyrics which he put to music. Some we used in our worship meetings and some are probably best forgotten! Out of this partnership came a musical entitled '*In the Last Days*'. This was for the most part an enjoyable project which was performed in two venues and subsequently, with additional material written by others, had a third outing. It traced the life of Jesus from his death on the cross to the day of Pentecost and although not a box office hit, many lives were challenged. The task of producing a musical, even at an amateur level, proved most challenging.

My involvement with the Boys Brigade was coming to an end. The final summer camp that I attended was at Sidmouth in East Devon. This week was during the annual Folk Festival and it seemed to me that it would make a wonderful place to take a team from the church on a mission trip. We linked with the YMCA in Sidmouth and had a wonderful week of mission and made many friends. The following year, joined by a team from Youth With A Mission, we returned to Sidmouth and held a very fruitful mission and some twenty-seven people made a response to the gospel.

Following this mission, which was an amazingly powerful introduction to spiritual warfare, I became great friends with John who was leading the work at the YMCA. I became a regular visitor to Sidmouth. I had some limited experience of demonic activity through my leadership of the church but the experiences that were to follow in confronting the forces of darkness were like transferring from Division 2 up to the Premier League. I am extremely thankful for the teaching of John

Wimber, who at that time was teaching the church about signs and wonders and how these can transform personal evangelism and promote church growth. It was at one of these conferences that I experienced the most significant healing I had seen up to that date. As we were queueing for refreshments the man in front of me revealed that he was deaf in one ear. He told me that his father and his grandfather had suffered the same deafness. The Holy Spirit led me to pray to break the hereditary spirit that was causing this deafness. (Spiritual gift- word of knowledge). He was instantly healed. It was another milestone in my understanding that led me into a life of working with the Lord in spiritual gifts. The Bible teaches very clearly that signs and wonders should accompany believers. (Mark 16:15-20).

Ephesians 6:12 reads *'We do not wrestle against flesh and blood, but against principalities, against powers, against the rulers of the darkness of this age, against spiritual hosts of wickedness in the heavenly places'*. Among those who were saved at the missions, and especially those at Sidmouth, several were troubled spiritually and in addition to receiving the salvation of Jesus Christ, we were also able to deliver them into the true freedom that Jesus brings. Not least of these was Tracey (name changed). This poor teenager had been dedicated to Satan as a child and had subsequently suffered severe physical, emotional and sexual abuse and particularly in satanic rituals. She was in an unbelievable mess! On her nineteenth birthday she was to have been entered by her coven into a competition for Queen of the Witches on Dartmoor. She was supplied with drugs by her coven and was heavily addicted to both drugs and alcohol. She responded to the preaching one evening and gave her life to Jesus. That became the start of a tremendous spiritual battle for her soul.

Tracey was invited to London by one of the mission team for her own safety. However, the addictions remained enormously powerful and her behaviour was extremely erratic. Through the many unclean spirits that indwelt her the covens from her home were trying to woo her back. It was difficult for any of the church members to contain her behaviour and so I moved her into my flat. I spent six weeks sleeping on the floor of a friend's home. She made several suicide attempts and I was often called to the hospital to bring her home. One evening after one such attempt, I was called to Lewisham Hospital. She had taken about 60 tablets (paracetamol and aspirin) and been rushed to the emergency department. Although the remnants of the tablets were found in her stomach, when the hospital ran tests, her blood was miraculously free from the presence of these drugs. On driving her home from this amazing intervention by God, she simply turned to me and said, *"I think this is now the time for my deliverance!"*

It is neither conventional nor recommended practice for a man to be alone with a lady for deliverance prayer and especially at night, but this was without doubt God's timing. That night Tracey was set free from the oppression of a multitude of evil spirits. It was a most amazing power encounter demonstrating that the power of God is infinitely greater than the powers of darkness. There was a multitude of these dark spirits, which had been tormenting her for many years, that fled at the name of Jesus. I do not wish to sensationalise what happened that night. I will simply quote Philippians 2:9:10 which states, *"God has given Jesus the Name above all names that at the name of Jesus every knee should bow!"* He certainly proved his power throughout that night.

Whilst being set free spiritually there were still many emotional and psychological hurdles to be overcome and we were able to find the right support for her. As part of her repentance she drew a map of the area around Sidmouth pointing out all the sites, mainly in the woodlands, where the covens and Satan worshippers met. I took a week's holiday and armed with this map found the places of darkness that they used and 'consecrated' them, thus rendering them unusable. During this week, John and I entered into a time of prayer and spiritual warfare on the seafront, and as we prayed a most violent storm arose. God was in this storm and we heard some days later that two of the covens around Sidmouth had folded and moved away. When we are truly born again of the Spirit of God we have no reason to fear these powers of darkness.

As the Bible says, *"The one who is in you is greater than the one who is in the world!"* (1 John 4:4)

My local football team is Charlton Athletic. Whilst never a fanatic I have always followed them since a boy. When I was a boy they would open the gates at half-time and let the local lads in for nothing to watch the second half and I have remained loyal ever since. Whilst walking near the ground one evening after an evening match at The Valley, I was aware of a violent and angry atmosphere on the streets. I decided I did not want these spiritual entities in my home area and so I started to pray that the spirits of violence and anger would leave the area. A few weeks later the whole football team left the ground for financial reasons and played at a nearby ground, Crystal Palace. Several people accused me of praying the football team out of the area. I replied that I had done no such thing! I simply prayed for the violent spirits to leave. It was not my fault that when they left the took the football team with them!

When I started the Charlton and Blackheath Christian Fellowship I knew that I would only be able to lead them so far. My calling as an evangelist was greater in me. I loved the Fellowship with all of its challenges but the desire of my heart and my ministry was becoming less 'to the church' and more 'from the church'. For about five years I poured my heart and soul into the fellowship and would have found it almost impossible to give it up if it were not for a certain set of circumstances which were triggered by the betrayal from a man that I trusted. It is not beneficial to go into those circumstances, but they eventually led to my stepping out of pastoral responsibility although at that time I remained in eldership.

I took every opportunity to share the good news of Jesus. I met a dear brother, Peter, who was a regular street preacher and it was not long before I joined him every Saturday morning in Woolwich. Through this work we met many interesting characters. Two of them were homeless and stayed with me for a short time. The first was Sean. He was Irish and worked on the building sites. He was alcoholic when we met him but when he responded to the gospel the Holy Spirit gave him power and broke his addiction. He lived with me for several weeks. His stature was commensurate with his work as a labourer but free from alcohol he was what I called a gentle giant. He was having trouble with the law which we were able to settle and the only house rule that I gave him was no alcohol in the house either inside him or in his hands. One Friday evening, fairly late at night, he came knocking at the door and he had started drinking again. He refused to come in and said he would sleep on the steps of the church. I could not persuade him to receive the second chance I offered him. He did at least accept a blanket from me. I did not hear much from him for some time and then learned that the alcohol addiction had taken hold of him again and in a drunken haze he had killed the man who had subsequently given him a home. He served a ten-year prison sentence for manslaughter. I did visit him a couple of times in prison and he had absolutely no recollection of killing his landlord. The last I heard he was assisting the prison chaplain. I do not know what became of him.

Billy was a different character. He had a heroin addiction and with the help of a local doctor I was able to get him on a course of methadone. He was a chirpy Glaswegian and earned good money busking with his guitar. Because of the erratic behaviour of addicts, I had extremely strict rules if he wished to live in my home. He kicked against these and one day on a bus he started talking to a stranger who unbeknown to him was known to me. During this conversation he said to my friend, "*I am living with a man who is too strict with me. You wouldn't happen to know of someone that I might stay with!*" I would love to have been a fly on the wall when the reply came, "*There is only one person I know who may be able to help you - his name is Stan Gain!*" Of all the people that he could have spoken to! Surely the Lord was in that conversation. Again, I was able to find a rehab for him in Scotland, but this failed. Ten days later he was again knocking at my door. It was tough for me but I had to turn him away telling him that when he genuinely wanted to be free to come back to me again. It can be difficult, but sometimes tough love is the only true way to help someone.

Through the sharing of the work of preaching in Woolwich, Peter and I became very close friends. When he had the opportunity to go to Kenya I was able to help him with the cost. He had a wonderful time working with George Opara who at that time lived in the shadow of Mount Elgon in a village called Lunyu. Unfortunately, while he was there, Peter contracted a viral disease. He never fully recovered and was not able to fulfil his promise to George to make a return visit. He had sent me a letter from Kenya which arrived after his return to London! One phrase in that letter almost jumped off the page and I knew it was a word from God. It simply said, '*Stan, you must come out here.*'

Little did I know that in a few short months I too would be on a flight to Nairobi, something which changed the course of my life from pastoral ministry to missionary evangelism and teaching. My adventure of faith was continuing and expanding. How grateful I was that the Lord had put me through such an intense five years of training in the life of the Holy Spirit.

Chapter 3

A Mighty Wind

"You know that people are fasting for us today!" said Marcus with a smile on his face as we tucked in to a good steak dinner on a Sudan Air flight into Khartoum. As Peter had been unable to fulfil his promise to return to Kenya, I was going in his place and Marcus accompanied me. We were met at Nairobi airport by George Opara and spent our first night in Africa in the Terminal Hotel. I was unsure if this name was prophetic as there was a spider on the wall, bigger and more evil looking than any spider I had ever seen before. Every time we turned off the lights the floor was crawling with cockroaches! Over the years I developed my own rating system for African hotels in the same way that hotels in the West are rated by stars. Instead of stars I use cockroaches, the worst hotel earning a five-cockroach rating. With hindsight, I would have given this hotel a rating of only two cockroaches, but this was my first night in Africa! However, we survived the night and next morning found ourselves on a very African bus travelling on very African roads to Kitale, a very African town. After a meal we went on to Liyavo village where George now lived on a five-acre plot of land. For most of my life I have lived in London but the noise in the African countryside was far noisier. I was not sure if I would ever sleep because of the sound of the crickets, frogs and un-known and unseen insects. I eventually fell asleep only to be woken at about four in the morning by the crowing of a cockerel sat right outside my bedroom.

Everything was a new experience but I was really excited when I saw the schedule, which included meetings on most days. The spirit of revival travelled with us and we saw many powerful situations from the hand of God. I was, as I still am, learning to move in signs and wonders. On our first morning we were taken to the home of Hetty, a missionary lady from the Netherlands. She was worryingly sick with malaria. We laid hands on her and as we prayed she suddenly ran out of the house and was violently sick. She looked much worse after we had prayed, and I wondered whether maybe this was not my ministry after all! However, the following day as we set out to travel, she jumped into the back of the truck with us in full health and gave testimony to the healing power of Jesus at the meetings we held that day.

Vitalis was one of George's pastors and he became one of my greatest friends. He was a mechanic and I soon learned that his gift would become essential as we travelled in a decaying, old and very African truck. One morning we loaded the truck with supplies and about twelve people and set off for a small village in Busia on the Ugandan border called Dirakho. Vitalis and Pastor Gabriel had visited Dirakho a few months earlier to plant a new church. They met with little success until at one home they prayed for a lady who was severely sick and unable to walk. She was instantly healed and as a consequence the church was started because of her testimony to such a great healing. We held several meetings under a huge avocado tree preaching in competition with extremely noisy cicadas but saw many people respond for salvation and healing. On one evening we went to the river Sio and baptised many people. Another church had been planted in a nearby village and during the meeting they held a fundraising for the building of a new church. I was touched to see how generously these people gave, not gifts of money, but of eggs, chickens, maize, rice and cassava. Although they had just a little to give they danced and sang as they gave generously from what little they had. On a subsequent visit I was delighted to see that the building had been completed.

This was to us a great adventure as we moved on to another small village called Sudi. I felt almost like royalty when we were met about a mile from the village and escorted all the way back by about a hundred people dancing, singing and praising God. This was another new village church and the host was an evangelist called Albert. He had many children and they formed a wonderful choir singing and dancing traditional songs. I later understood why Albert had so many children. On our first evening, I was sitting in his home when he came in and introduced a lady as his wife. I greeted her politely. He then introduced a second lady as his wife!

28

Then a third and then a fourth. I had not come across polygamy until now but hope I was able to keep my facial expression clear even though my mind was quickly computing this new situation! Although the church was on his land, the Bible does not allow a pastor to have more than one wife. However, when it came time to pray for Albert we prayed that he would be as fruitful as an evangelist as he was as a father. The last I heard he had over fifty children. On one flight to Nairobi I sat next to a young lady who was one of 254 children. Her father had 22 wives!

On our return to Liyavo, we had one of our many mechanical failures. I was amazed to see Vitalis at work on one of these breakdowns. The only tool that we were carrying was a hammer and yet he was able to strip down the carburettor and clean the valves with a piece of grass, reassemble the whole thing and put it back under the bonnet. To my amazement the vehicle started and we were able to reach home. I have learned how resourceful people can be even when they appear to have no resources. We really do take so much for granted in the West.

Another memorable journey on this trip was to Lunyu. This was the village where Peter had stayed and pastor Protus had built a fine church building. It was a long journey and sitting hot, dusty and bouncing around in the back of an open truck under a hot sun left me feeling somewhat grumpy! I was beginning to think of home and wondering why I had bothered to come to Kenya when God clearly spoke to my heart and said, *"Stan, are you content?"* I felt this was not the best time to ask such a question. I began to consider my circumstances. I was serving God; I had met some wonderful people; I had seen many people saved and healed; I was preaching at least once every day and had truly seen the power of God at work. I could only give one answer, *"Yes, Lord! I am content!"* From that moment all the circumstances that made me feel grumpy did not seem so bad and I arrived at the church enthusiastically ready to preach. I learned a valuable lesson on that journey that our faith does not depend on our circumstances or our material possessions but is truly found in Jesus.

The report of the Day of Pentecost recorded in Acts chapter 2 reads, *"When the Day of Pentecost had fully come, they were all with one accord in one place. And suddenly there came a sound from heaven, as of a rushing mighty wind, and it filled the whole house where they were sitting."* When the time came to preach I had a message ready to share but as I stood I felt the Lord prompting me to preach a completely different word. I have learned to be obedient to such promptings and preached a message about returning fully to the values of biblical doctrine. As always at these meetings we invited people to receive salvation.

As I raised my hands to pray for those who had responded a violent wind suddenly blew through the whole church. The weather outside was calm and sunny but this wind blowing through the church was immensely powerful and although unaware of the time, I estimate it lasted well over an hour. Such was the noise and the force of this wind that many people who had not been at the meeting came running to the church seeking salvation. It was awesome! We had been planning to go to the river to baptise several people but God intervened and changed our plan. It was a lesson for me to understand that when ministering in any situation it is important to be flexible and listen to the voice of the Holy Spirit! If we wish to see revival, we must give up our pre-set programmes, timetables and agendas. As much as I long to see God move in this power again, to date this has been my only true 'Pentecost wind' experience. It is quite ironic that on the same day, the Great Storm of 1987 battered the UK, with winds of up to 120 mph and around 15 million trees were blown over. I prefer the wind of the Holy Spirit. It is more powerful but does not wreak destruction!

This first mission trip to Kenya was over too soon and we found ourselves once again on the Akamba bus bouncing back to Nairobi on the dusty roads and an appointment with the two-cockroach hotel. We said goodbye to George at the airport and went in to find our flight back to Khartoum and on to London. To our dismay our flight was not listed on the departure board and there was no sign of any representative of Sudan Air. We were advised to go to the office of Kenyan Airways, the host airline. The manager was very apologetic and said they had a flight to London but it was already overbooked. I thanked him and left his office with Marcus and we sat in the airport. As we left I felt a surge of faith rise in me and said to Marcus, *"Do not worry, we are going home. We have spent a month serving the Lord and he will not let us down."* (Spiritual gift - the word of faith). We had no money, no valid ticket and no flight home but I was confident in the promises of God. Surprisingly, God proved His faithfulness after a quite short time. The Kenya Airways manager came and found us sitting in the airport and told us to bring our tickets to his office. He informed us that those who were booked to London on the Sudan Air flight had been transferred to his flight. We looked down the list of passengers but our names were not listed. Once again, I thanked him, and we resumed our wait in the airport and I again said to Marcus, *"Marcus, we are going home!"* He gave me an old-fashioned look but said nothing.

Shortly afterwards the manager came again and found us and said as before to bring our tickets to his office. When we got there, he got on the phone to the check-in desk and instructed them to take our tickets and put us on standby. As before, I thanked him and we did as he had suggested. However, when we got to the check-in desk we were told that they could not accept our tickets as they were not transferable to another airline. Once again I confirmed to Marcus that we were going home. So back we went again to Kenyan Airways. The manager again got on the phone and told the check-in desk that without fail they should accept our tickets and put us on <u>priority</u> standby. This they did, telling us to return to the desk at 12.30. I thought they were joking as the flight was due to leave at midnight but he assured me that the flight was delayed. At about 12:10 he called our names and gave us our boarding passes. We arrived in London on a direct flight six hours ahead of the scheduled time of Sudan Air. This was a great lesson in faith for us and I learned a massive lesson in trusting God and his promises. I have already mentioned Rees Howell, who was used mightily in the Welsh revival. He used to say that the promises of God *'were better than current coin'*! In other words, it is better to trust in the Lord than in your pocket.

It has often been said that once you have been to Africa it gets into your blood. This was certainly true for me and in about six months I was back in the Terminal Hotel in Nairobi awaiting a bus to take us back to Kitale and many new adventures. On this trip I was accompanied by a young man named Jan (pronounced Yan). As with Marcus it was good to have someone travelling with me and Jan proved to be a great travelling companion. Having had a similar road trip to Liyavo, I was delighted to see on arrival that once again we had a very full schedule. We were to meet many old friends and make many new ones too. The only difference was that although Vitalis was to travel with us I was now appointed the driver. I learned very quickly that this was in case we were stopped by the police. If they saw a white man (mzungu) driving there was less chance of being stopped! I soon understood this as when I started to drive I realised that the brakes needed pumping several times before they engaged and the steering wheel had about 5 inches play. However, I was told that it was a good vehicle by African standards. My subsequent experience confirmed to me that this was indeed a good vehicle by African standards.

Whilst the schedule on this trip was similar the high points were significantly different. We visited Dirakho again and found the church was growing both numerically and spiritually. Since these early visits Dirakho has always had a special place in my heart and I am still in touch with the church. Through Starfish Christian Trust which came to be formed many years later we are still supporting the teachers of a school whose pupils are predominantly orphans of the HIV/AIDS virus. About 5 miles away another church had been planted and the spirit of revival was continuing. This church was also without doubt on fire for the Lord. When the power of God is present there is no knowing what He will do in a meeting. On one occasion while I was preaching I suddenly noticed a girl writhing on the floor like a snake and her tongue was moving in and out in a snake-like manner. I later learned that this was a spirit of divination, sometimes called a spirit of Python, a similar spirit to that which the Apostle Paul encountered in Acts 16:16. She was wonderfully delivered from this spirit. It is no surprise to know that witchcraft is extremely common in Africa.

32

Many people, indeed, many Christians do not have an understanding that evil spirits can severely influence the thoughts and behaviour of ordinary men and women. Whilst I do not always use the term 'demon possessed', preferring to use the word demonised, there is no doubt that men and women can be overcome and oppressed by such evil spirits. They did not all suddenly disappear when Jesus went back to heaven. Modern empirical thinking will in most cases rationalise the effects that such spirits can have on an individual. It is not just in the uneducated developing world that such manifestations occur but also in our own sophisticated Western culture. For the most part, however, it is not recognised for what it is in the West.

It was on this trip to Dirakho that I succumbed to malaria for the first time. We were staying in an empty shop with no chance of protecting ourselves from the clouds of mosquitoes that lived in the area. We were quite close to the river Nzoia which separated Kenya from Uganda and this was a huge breeding ground. We were sleeping on rough mattresses on the floor. A few days later I was violently sick and was rushed to the Mission Hospital at Nangina where I was told that the strain of malaria in that area was chloroquine resistant. I was hallucinating badly and I guess that would explain why I was the only one who could see the dozens of monkeys and lynxes all around us! On my return to Dirakho I asked the team travelling with us to pray for me and settled on my mattress for the night. When I awoke the next morning the malaria had lifted from me completely. The Lord had healed me. We had been praying for the sick throughout our travels and I guess this was my turn!

On one occasion I was asked to visit a home to pray for a lady who was obviously extremely sick. As I entered the home I discerned a strong spirit of witchcraft and the lady acknowledged she was involved with this occult practice. (spiritual gift – discerning of spirits). Before I could pray for her I asked her if she would renounce her witchcraft but she would not. I was concerned that if this spirit was cast out that the warning of Jesus in Luke 11:26 might be fulfilled. Jesus warned that if after a spirit is cast out the 'empty space' is not filled with the Holy Spirit that it could be re-inhabited by more spirits than had left! For this lady I was concerned that unless she was filled with the Holy Spirit her last state would be worse than her first. I could only make a general prayer for her. I told her that on the day she renounced witchcraft and received Jesus she would be healed.

After one meeting we went down to the River Nzoia where over fifty people were ready to be baptised. At the end of meeting we prayed for people who wished to be filled with the Holy Spirit. I was led to tell those who were to be baptised in water to hold back as they would receive the Holy Spirit baptism as they came out of the water. What a powerful gathering it was at the river that afternoon. Some almost exploded out of the water when we immersed them. Others left the river speaking and praising God in tongues. (Spiritual gift - speaking in tongues). One young man came into the river and I discerned he had deep spiritual problems. As he approached, I said to Jan to watch as God was going to do something extremely powerful in his life. After immersing him, we lifted him out of the water and he was fully unconscious. I thought at first that he was dead! I was not sure what this was at first but on praying for him he fully recovered and was wonderfully delivered and filled with the Holy Spirit. On a later visit I was delighted to see that he was now pastoring a new church.

Whenever we went to the river or to Lake Victoria to baptise there was always a prayer to protect those in the water from disease. On one occasion when baptising, about 50 feet up the river there was a herd of cows doing what cows do in the water! Another time we were travelling to Lunyu again to baptise several people. Before we reached the river we stopped at a house and I saw George give some money to the owner. I am naturally curious and so I asked him what the reason for this was. He told me that a family member had been bitten by a snake whilst in the river and that the money was to pay for his medical bills. *"Is that the river that Jan and I are going into to baptise these people?"* *"Yes,"* he replied with an almost cheeky grin, *"We are more than conquerors!"* It was not until we had finished baptising and were changing into dry clothes that I said to

Jan, *"Let me tell you a story of a man, a river and a snake!"* He gave me a rather old-fashioned look, but we laughed about it on the road back home.

The work of The Lord's Ministry, the work that George had started, was growing very rapidly. George had given one acre from his land for the building of a church. I was delighted on returning home to Charlton and Blackheath Christian Fellowship to hear that they had agreed to fund the construction. It took two attempts at building this church as the rains, which often cause great destruction, under-mined the foundations before the roof could be properly secured. I was privileged on a later visit to be at the church opening. This was a great celebration especially as The Lord's Ministry had also received official registration as a ministry from the Kenyan Government.

As the vision grew, it was agreed that we would together finance the building of an orphanage at Centa Kwanza. I have always had a spirit of adventure and having seen the beauty of Mount Kilimanjaro from Tsavo National Park saw my chance to climb. I raised a considerable amount in sponsorship. Climbing it was much tougher than I thought and is probably the hardest physical thing that I have done in my whole life. Setting out from Moshi in Tanzania, we arrived at base camp on the first day at about 12,000 feet. Thankfully, we had a guide and porters so all we needed to carry was our water. This we carried around our waist under our clothing to stop it freezing as we reached a higher altitude. By the time we reached the second base at 15,000 feet the altitude was having a great effect and we could only walk at a snail's pace. At midnight, we set off for a slower than a snail's pace climb and reached Gilman's Point on the edge of the crater of the volcano to see the sun rise over the clouds. As the sun rose higher its rays hit a glacier and this is one of the most beautiful things I have ever seen. I may not have been the first but I named it the Crystal Cathedral! It took a long time to trudge on to Uhuru Peak, but I arrived with a great sense of achievement, not just for conquering the mountain, but for raising almost enough money in sponsorship to build the orphanage.

The timing of this second visit was during a rainy season and it was impossible to avoid getting mud everywhere! On one night there was a particularly heavy rainstorm and the next morning Vitalis came to collect us and his face was unusually sad. Apparently this storm had destroyed his maize crop. Sometimes a word of faith will rise in a believer and on this occasion, I said to Vitalis, *"Do not worry! You have given many weeks to help us and serve the Lord. He will honour your service and you will not lose out because of this."* I thought nothing more of this until about three weeks later on a sunny morning we were driving close to Vitalis's home. He and George were talking in Swahili and I was in my own world looking out of the window when Vitalis said to me, *"Brother Stan, the Lord has answered your prayer."* I was not sure what he meant but he continued *"Look at how the maize has recovered!"* When he said this I looked at the fields of maize and they were completely recovered. I had seen the maize fields after the storm and now there was absolutely no sign of damage, not just on his land but in the whole area of Namanjalala where he lived. The leaves which had been torn to shreds and hanging limply were completely restored. This was another great lesson as I was learning to live by faith. Nothing is impossible to him who believes (Everything is HIMpossible!). He later told me that his harvest of maize that year was much greater than he had ever experienced before.

Africa had won my heart. Little did I know at that time that I would travel to Nairobi about fifty times over the years! I probably spent more than five years of my life in Africa in total. I was still the pastor at Charlton and Blackheath Christian Fellowship and was learning that a pastor (shepherd) should stay with his sheep. Long periods away sometimes meant that on my return there were difficulties to resolve. After this second trip to Kenya I decided that I needed a holiday and what could be a more natural holiday for an evangelist than to lead a team to the Soviet Union?

Chapter 4

Hair Driers!

Operation Mobilisation has over the years had a wonderful world-wide ministry. In addition to its ministry with hospital ships it has also encouraged people to venture on short and medium-term mission trips. I was in need of a break from pastoral ministry and I decided to enrol at an OM conference in Brussels. After a three-day conference, the delegates were then sent on a short-term mission to different areas of Europe. I duly filled in my application and several days later I received a phone call asking if I would be prepared to be a team leader and to lead a short-term mission to the Soviet Union. Never being one to duck a challenge, I naturally accepted.

Following the conference, I was introduced to the team who came from five different countries. We were given a large Ford Transit van for our journey which was packed tightly, not only with food and camping equipment but about 30,000 pieces of Christian literature to be distributed on our travels. It was a fairly uneventful journey through Germany and Poland. We all had the necessary visas and it was still fairly tense as we crossed from East to West Germany through the infamous Checkpoint Charlie in Berlin. It seemed quite intimidating crossing this vast no man's land. It was a vast area completely denuded of vegetation et cetera and it is amazing to think that so many risked their lives, some succeeding to get from East to West. But we got through without incident. We knew that there were potential difficulties at the Soviet border as we were carrying the large quantities of Christian literature. Although the terms *glasnost* and *perestroika* were coming into the news, it was still highly illegal to take such literature into the Soviet Union. However, God performed an unusual miracle that enabled us to cross the border without problems and, miraculously, without the vehicle even being searched. Here we learn another lesson in the power of prayer. We knew the approximate time that we would cross into the Soviet Union and had many people praying for us.

As our turn came at the border we had to drive across an inspection pit, similar to those used in garages to inspect the underside of vehicles. This one was about thirty feet long. Initially we stopped and presented our passports and visas to the appropriate authorities and we then had to drive along the inspection pit so that our vehicle could be examined. The border guard was just reaching out his hand to open the rear doors and inspect our luggage, a very tense moment, when the miracle happened. I got out of the vehicle and nervously walked to the back. I looked up across a barren area and saw a gleaming white Lada car with sparkling chrome driving straight towards us. It was almost dazzling in the sunlight. There appeared to be no purpose to his driving in our direction and it did not stop until it had driven nose first into the inspection pit behind us with a very loud bang. This naturally caused a great commotion and it was all hands on deck to lift the vehicle from the pit. Once this had been done our border guard came back to us, returned our passports, closed the now open rear doors of our vehicle and waved us through without an inspection! The Lada car has over the years been the butt of many jokes but the Lord has shown that he too has a sense of humour by choosing such an amusing way to see us safely into the Soviet Union. (Oh yes! What is the difference between a Lada and a golf ball? You can drive a golf ball 200 yards!)

We still had an exceptionally long and tiring drive to reach Kiev but eventually reached the Intourist campsite where we gratefully erected our tents before making contact with Andrei who was to be our guide and interpreter. We had no choice but to continue driving as the visitor to the Soviet Union at that time had no option but to book their visits through Intourist, a branch of the dreaded KGB. Our only permitted destination was the campsite in Kiev. After much needed sleep Andrei took us to the town of Boyarka to meet Pastor Kozachuck and his wife with whom we were mainly to work. It was a humbling experience to meet them. Pastor Kozachuck had kept an illegal printing press in his basement for the production of Christian literature. He had been caught by the Soviet authorities and had spent several years in a Siberian prison. As I have since often found, those who experience genuine persecution for their faith exude and reflect the character of Jesus and the fruit of the Holy Spirit in great abundance. The pastor and his wife were no exception and were among the humblest of people I have met. Mrs Kozachuk must have been well over 70 years old but she had the face of an angel. On one occasion I asked her how sad she must have been when her husband was imprisoned. She just smiled, looked up and said she was proud of her husband and privileged to be able to be persecuted together for sharing their Christian faith.

I had on a previous occasion listened to a Romanian pastor, Richard Wurmbrand. He had spent some fourteen years in a Romanian prison, again, simply because of his faith. Although he appeared very frail in his body, when he spoke the power of God fell in the church. He wrote a book entitled *Tortured for Christ*. In the book he recounts how he was regularly beaten for sharing the gospel in the prison. One of his quotes has remained with me and I paraphrase, *"Every time we preached the prison guards would beat us. Therefore, everyone was happy! We were happy to be preaching and they were happy to beat us."* Such wonderful people of God are such a challenge to our 'soft' Christianity.

I have been privileged to meet so many awesome, yet humble, men and women of God. I cannot recall how many times I have listened to preachers and teachers quote from Revelation 12:11. *"And they overcame him (the devil) by the blood of the Lamb and by the word of their testimony..."* Our soft Western Christianity likes this verse but it does not stop there. The second half of the verse reads *"and they did not love their lives even unto the death"*. This is not so popular and probably too challenging, but these are the three ways in which we overcome, not just the two! I pray that God will put back the fire into the belly of our preachers so that the fire of God will truly fall.

We were taken to many places including educational establishments, workers cooperatives and of course churches to share the love of Jesus. I am always humbled by the humility of the many pastors with whom I have worked. One evening, on a subsequent visit, I found myself sat around a table with eight Soviet pastors all of whom had been imprisoned simply for their faith. I wanted to sit at their feet and listen to their stories but it was they who insisted that I shared with them. At the time of the collapse of the Berlin Wall I heard many Western Christians almost being self-congratulatory for their prayer that communism would fall. Believe me, those on the eastern side of the Wall were praying with much more fervency!

Over many years of travel to many places, I have visited many children's homes and orphanages. The orphanage in Boyarka was the first that I visited in a communist country. It almost broke my heart when a small and handsome young boy of about three years of age looked up at me with hope in his eyes as he asked, "*Abba? Abba?*" He was asking in his way, "*Are you my father? Have you come to take me home?*" To have picked him up would have raised tremendous hope in his little heart which would probably have been further broken when he was again put down. It was with great difficulty that I ignored his cry. Believe me, when I got back home and remembered his little face I shed a few tears myself. To their credit this orphanage was exceptionally clean and the children did look to be well cared for. In my later travels to Romania and Albania I saw children living in heart-breaking conditions.

On the second night in our small igloo tents we became soaked through as the most torrential rain fell through the night. The Lord taught me two great lessons about prayer the next morning. We were huddled in the driest of our tents for our morning prayer and for all that we were facing in bringing the gospel to the Soviet Union. I was amazed that one of the girls prayed for somewhere dry to sleep and a place that they could plug in their hair dryers! To me it seemed such a trivial thing but to them it was important and if it was important to them it was also important to God. That day we set off for another day of adventure. This was to include a visit to the local prison. Andrei had obtained permission for one of the team to go into the prison and talk with the prisoners. Being the team leader, I was nominated, and I was taken into a room full of very tough-looking men. Andrei was called away and I was left in the locked room with them. I was unable to communicate with the men except to use some childishly simple and basic sign language. After about forty-five minutes Andrei had not returned and I began to wonder whether the authorities were unhappy that we were there to promote Christianity. I was locked in this prison room with no English speaker to tell me what was happening. I was heartily relieved when after what seemed like an interminable time he returned, and I was able to speak with the men about Jesus.

After a full day we returned to the campsite ready for a good night's rest. Imagine our consternation when we arrived at the site to discover that every piece of our equipment had disappeared except for one tea towel hanging in the bushes. Intourist, through whom all visits to the Soviet Union were arranged was a branch of the KGB. This campsite, therefore, was also a part of their domain and we began to wonder what this could mean. We went to the office and a very officious lady eventually explained that our equipment had been 'mistakenly' packed up by the site manager who had left on vacation for three days and he had sealed it. As he was the one who had sealed it he was the only one who could unseal it. There was nothing that she could do! My anger was aroused and although I knew her to be a KGB officer I was not going to let this rest. After much argument she started to walk away from me into a private area. I followed her and shouted after her, "*Don't you dare walk away from me. You may treat your own people this way, but we are visitors in your country. In our team we have people from five nations and if our belongings are not returned to us I will contact all five embassies. I know your name.*" Although it was now late in the day this seemed to have the desired effect. That night we were given two dry chalets to stay in… and the girls had somewhere to plug in their hairdryers! We stayed in these chalets for the rest of our stay, dry and warm and our property was returned to us intact although probably not before it had been inspected. Thankfully the literature was in the vehicle.

Overall, it was a tough trip and we rested in Berlin for a couple of days before returning to Brussels to debrief. I knew that I was to return to Soviet Union again and in discussions with Andrei he suggested that the next time I should come in a less conspicuous vehicle! This I did and the way that the Lord provided was again quite exciting.

Around this time, John Wimber was holding a conference about prayer in Brighton which I attended. One of the sessions was teaching about how we should ask the Lord for our needs. At the end of this session he told us all to stand and to ask the Lord for a specific need to be supplied. By this time, I was growing in the concept of 'living by faith' and trusting the Lord to provide my needs. He had taught me to be content in whatever my circumstances whilst on the road to Lunyu in Africa. As I stood I considered for a while and was genuine in saying to the Lord, *"I do not have any needs!"* To my surprise He replied, *"Ask me for a car."* I felt I had nothing to lose and so I asked the Lord for a *reliable* car. Thinking about it later the thought occurred that the Lord would not provide an unreliable car. When I got home I thought no more about it until about ten days later a friend approached me and said that he believed that I needed a car and handed me a cheque which enabled me to buy what turned out to be an extremely reliable car. Some people laughed at the car that I bought but, bearing in mind that Andrei had suggested I return in a less conspicuous car, I found myself buying a Lada! In spite of the jokes, (What do you call a Lada with twin exhaust pipes? A wheelbarrow!) it turned out to be extremely reliable, as I had asked. It took me overland from the UK to the Soviet Union towing a trailer on three occasions and twice to Romania. The Lord is surely faithful to his word. The only problem I had on all these trips was a puncture in the wheel of the trailer.

By the time of my second visit, President Gorbachev was further relaxing the harshness of communism and the words *'glasnost'* and *'perestroika'* (meaning openness and restructuring) were becoming more common. Now with my reliable vehicle and a trailer packed with Bibles, tools, clothes and sewing machines I set off for a second visit to Boyarka. This time, I had few problems at the border and the openness meant that I was able to travel much more freely although still under the watchful eye of Intourist. I could only stay at the Intourist hotel into which I had been booked. It was a long journey and at about midnight, still a long way from my destination, a big black Soviet car pulled alongside me looking very menacing indeed. I once again resorted to my well used short and effective prayer "H E L P!" This was answered in a very strange way. My car accelerated away at high-speed leaving this menacing vehicle far behind. I arrived at my destination at about two in the morning, but I was safe.

This incident reminded me of a time when I was with Mike, one of the elders of my church. We were in his car travelling down Charlton Road in London. Suddenly a car pulled out from behind a bus at great speed heading straight towards us. There was no room for it to pass us and yet in an instant it was behind us. Neither of us knew what had happened, but we both agreed that the only explanation was the protection of the Lord. We often talk about guardian angels and ministering angels and I am so glad they travel with me wherever I go.

I was away for a total of seven weeks and have to this day never had more meetings than I had at that time. Pastor Kozachuck was delighted to see me again because, as he expressed it, I was the first Westerner to visit his town. He had been severely persecuted and imprisoned by the communists because of his faith but '*glasnost*' enabled him to move freely. Consequently, he took me to just about every educational establishment, hospital, factory, and even the local police and KGB! I even have a book presented to me and signed by the officers of the KGB! He was able to arrange meetings in so many places because he had the first Western visitor in his church. This raised his status as the pastor of what had been an unregistered Baptist church. In each of these meetings I would spend half my time talking about education or healthcare etc. as appropriate and the other half preaching the gospel. This also became a pattern in my subsequent visits. Now, after my visit, the door was open for Pastor Kozachuck to freely take the gospel all around Boyarka and beyond.

What was particularly interesting was that in many non-communist countries most people understand the existence of God - whether or not they particularly follow Him. When preaching in the West, there is usually no need to explain that God exists. Here, in communist Soviet Union, the starting point was to literally go back to basics. Most people had been told all their lives by the Communist authorities that God does not exist. This needed to be challenged before the truth of the gospel could be explained. It was a great experience to be able to challenge the Communist teaching that, *"There is no God!"* For many it was as if a light had been turned on. Ecclesiastes 3:11 states that *"God has set eternity into the hearts of men."* People were touching base, as it were, with that which God had placed within them. Interestingly many of the older people made comments to the effect that they remembered their grandparents speaking of these things. Even now, I find it difficult to imagine a world without the knowledge of God.

On my second visit, Andrei was not always available to interpret. On one occasion they were able to find a lecturer from the local university who was prepared to act as my interpreter, but she had had no experience or contact with the church and was therefore, understandably, somewhat nervous about the task. However, before the meetings, I had a lengthy conversation with her to explain many Christian terms that she had never heard before. I could see that the Lord was working on her heart at this time. It was interesting travelling with her and one particular incident was instrumental in her coming to faith. I was standing with my hand wrapped around the doorjamb of our car as we were preparing to travel. Inadvertently, she shut the door on my fingers. She was amazed when I calmly stood there and asked her to open the door. There was absolutely no damage to my fingers and I had no pain. She could not believe her eyes. For the rest of the day she kept asking to see my undamaged fingers. It is amazing how God will use any and every situation if we trust and believe him. It took me back to an incident that had happened one evening many years before at the Boys Brigade Hall.

Sometimes, as we are reading the Bible, a particular verse or passage will speak directly to our hearts. It will jump out at us as if it has our name written all over it. On this occasion the Lord quickened such a verse to me from Psalm 22 – *'He guards all his bones; not one of them is broken.'* Although this verse is prophetic concerning Jesus on the cross at Calvary, I accepted this verse as a promise of God to myself. The next evening I was playing basketball with some lads at the hall. On one occasion I reached for the ball and it caught just my fingers and the middle finger on my right hand took the full force and looked severely broken. The devil will often challenge us and try to steal the word from us but I remembered the promise of the verse above. I held my fingers in my left hand and as I prayed my hand was fully restored! The next day I was carrying a heavy suitcase with absolutely no discomfort in that hand. It is only when we give more than mental assent to the Word of God and believe that what the Lord says he will do, he will do, that we will see its true power.

To return to the Russian interpreter, on my subsequent visit she was so eager to come and tell me that the incident with the car door had caused her to believe in God and she had given her life to Jesus. On this visit, the pastor of the Baptist church told me that the next day there was to be a wedding in the church and he invited me to "bless the couple!" I thought this would simply mean praying for them after he had married them. When working cross culturally we should never take anything for granted! It was a large church with two balconies that held about 3000 people and on Sunday morning at 11 o'clock at the start of the service the interpreter had not yet arrived. About ten minutes later she came and sat between me and the pastor. They spoke for a short time then she leaned across to me and said, "They are ready for you now." I was a little confused until she explained that I was to take the wedding service! With no preparation and absolutely no warning I found myself standing before the young bride and groom as I fumbled my way through what I remembered of the English wedding ceremony and vows. It seems that by the end of the ceremony everybody was happy to have witnessed an English wedding!

This was one of many situations where I have been taken completely unawares. When travelling with young Marcus on the first Africa trip, I decided to let him speak at one meeting and sat back expecting a 'morning off'! I was feeling quite relaxed by the end of his message and was thinking we were nearing the end of the service and lunch. I was taken by surprise when the pastor said, "Now let's hear what the other brother has to say." Once again I had to stand with no preparation and speak for about one hour. Thankfully, when we believe God's promises He will see us through. On another occasion I was taking a three-day seminar at Chwele in western Kenya and found myself teaching from the Sermon on the Mount. About halfway through the third session I realised that the teaching was new revelation to me – I had never heard this teaching before. Later, the Lord told me that I was never to worry that when I stood to speak I would have nothing to say. This promise has since carried me through many situations where I have since been put on the spot.

Most people will remember the tragedy of the Chernobyl nuclear power station. It affected the lives of many communities. The authorities had evacuated most of the people within a large radius of the power plant, but the Christian families were still living in the shadow of the disaster. An exclusion zone had been set for many miles around the plant, and I had the privilege of visiting a church within that exclusion zone. Everyone in the village had been evacuated except for the Christians. It was not permissible for me as a Westerner to travel in this area so leaving my trusty Lada behind we headed for the power station in a Soviet registered vehicle. To my consternation, I saw that all the fields in this area were being fully harvested. When I asked how this could be I was told that the food would be added to the general harvest in the area and beyond and basically no one would know of the contamination!

Andrei's church had collected provisions for these believers as they had no other viable means of support. As we got closer to our destination we passed through abandoned villages with high fences either side of the road to exclude anyone from staying or straying off the road.

Photography was of course prohibited, but we had a 'convenient' breakdown in one village and from under the bonnet of the car I was able to take some photos. We had a good church meeting and afterwards went to the pastor's house for fellowship. My strongest memory is of little Ula, a five-year-old girl who was in her mother's womb at the time of the nuclear meltdown. She was obviously mentally damaged by the radiation. She looked at me with great suspicion as she hid behind her mother. My only form of communication was to give her a smile and a wave. She ran at me with great enthusiasm and clung to me like a limpet. Although she was cared for she smelled strongly of urine but that seemed unimportant. This little lass had few friends and recognised my love for her and responded accordingly. I often wonder what became of this community and of dear little Ula.

On a visit to Belcy in Moldova, I was delighted to learn that prior to my arrival the church had taken delivery of several thousand Russian bibles. I was told that the Communist presses were no longer printing their propaganda. The United Bible Society in the UK had provided funds for the printing of these bibles, ironically on the very presses that had printed the literature declaring, 'there is no God'. It was indeed a privilege to be able to work with the church in the distribution of many hundreds of these bibles. I was asked if I would take some specimen copies of these back to the UBS. Over the years, many people had risked their lives smuggling bibles into the Soviet Union. I like to boast that I was the first person to 'smuggle' bibles out!

During my visits to the Soviet Union I was still also travelling to Kenya. In both of these countries I could see great need. My heart was to do as much as I could to alleviate at least a small part of that need. I started collecting all sorts of items to take with me to both places. I have mentioned that I hooked up a trailer behind my trusty Lada car and filled it with aid. Also at that time, we were working to develop The Lord's Ministry in Kenya. A dear friend donated a vehicle for use as a mobile clinic and we had seen about six village clinics opened. My front room at home began to look more like a warehouse than a place of relaxation.

One day, having returned from a road trip to the Soviet Union and a subsequent flight to Kenya with about seven full size cases laden with medical equipment I was feeling exhausted. I said to the Lord, "*I cannot cope with all this need!*" His immediate reply to me was, "*I didn't ask you to!*" In effect He was saying that the harvest is His responsibility and not mine. If He wanted me to work in one field one day and a different field on another that was all that was needed. It was a great relief to know that I was neither responsible to feed nor to rescue the world. A great burden lifted from me that day. I now pray according to Luke 10:2 that the Lord of the Harvest sends out labourers into His harvest.

I enjoyed the work of visiting the Soviet Union but it was extremely tiring. On a subsequent visit, lasting about seven weeks, I found I was speaking as many as seven times a day. Maybe starting at a polytechnic, going on to a university class followed by a local co-operative or police station. Most days ending with a church service. It was a real privilege to carry the name of Jesus and the message of salvation to so many who had no concept of God and I understand that many lives were changed as a consequence of these visits. However, after my fourth visit and an eventual serious mechanical problem with my trusty Lada, (Why does a Lada have a heated rear window? To keep your hands warm when you are pushing it!) I felt it time to pass on this work to another ministry. I had learned a great deal from these visits and they were certainly not my last to Communist Eastern Europe.

Chapter 5

So You Are Securitate?

Eastern Europe fascinated me. The Communist regimes were probably nowhere tighter than in Romania and Albania. I was invited to be a trustee for the Protekton Trust by a dear friend. Brian, who had set up the trust, was an expert and lecturer in hospital x-ray equipment. He had discovered that the machines that our own hospitals were discarding were far superior to those in use in Eastern Europe. He set up the trust which received the discarded equipment and the trust was able to transport them to mainly Romania and Albania. Of course, the churches in these countries were severely persecuted and the pastors could be arrested for any trivial thing. The Communist authorities desperately needed this equipment and by delivering it through the churches the pastors were allowed more freedom since any spares and repairs et cetera needed to be supplied through those churches. It was a great scheme which brought some relief to the persecuted church.

That is how I found myself on a flight to the Romanian capital, Bucharest, with a genuine x-ray engineer. My total knowledge of x-rays is that they produce funny pictures of our skeletons. Armed with this wealth of knowledge and experience I found myself in the hospital in Bucharest with the engineer. Needless to say the Securitate guys were everywhere and I was feeling quite insecure as I was looking at machines, copying serial numbers for no apparent reason and trying to appear as if I had a purpose for being there. I could not keep this up for long and so I sat down and a Securitate guy soon sat next to me and started asking me questions. Thankfully, he too knew nothing about x-ray equipment as he had trained as a lawyer, but under the Communist system took the job he was told to do! He was trying to work out who I really was and the only explanation came when he asked the question, *"So you are Securitate?"* I realised my opportunity. It appeared that their security system was about to work against them and give me clearance. I did not lie by admitting that this was the case but I gave him a wink and a wry smile which satisfied him. He took this to be a 'yes' and from there on I was one of them and had much more freedom and was able to visit the church.

This of itself was a surprising experience. I had expected to visit a small, perhaps underground church but found myself in an exceptionally large church and the sanctuary full to capacity. There were not many people in Romania that spoke English but the man sitting next to me was able to answer any questions I had about the service. The Spirit of God was powerfully evident. It helped me in forming an opinion that perhaps the churches in the West might benefit from a little persecution. In Eastern Europe in those days you did not go to church as a social club or to meet friends. The risk of arrest, persecution, imprisonment and torture was always there. It certainly meant that all those who attend the services are genuinely born again. I heard a story of a communist soldier who visited an underground church. He was fully armed and cocked his rifle and said that anybody who was not a Christian was free to leave. With the prospect of what looked to be at best arrest and at worst arrest, torture and possible death several of those present left. Once they were gone he rested his rifle against the wall and said he now knew that he was with true believers and joined in their fellowship.

Although there were hundreds of believers at this church, they had very few Bibles. During the service a young girl stood and was speaking for a long time in Romanian. I asked the man sitting next to me what she was saying. He told me that as most of the Christians do not have bibles, when they have access to one they learn it by heart. This young lady was reciting, as a Bible reading, several complete chapters of the Gospel of Matthew that she had committed to memory. He further explained that should she or any other believer be arrested and persecuted and had no access to the Word of God, it would be in their memory and they could not take that away from her. He added that when they got a Bible they broke it into several parts so that different members of the congregation could all have a part to memorise.

Security was extremely tight and everywhere we went we were very aware of the presence of Securitate agents. Even walking from the hospital to our hotel we were accompanied by one such. It was quite amusing in the hotel lobby because the agents were so obvious. Each wore a long leather jacket and sat reading a newspaper. Naturally, all the hotel rooms were bugged. At a meeting with some Swiss people who were staying at the hotel, we were told the following anecdote. One of them had had a birthday and he had somehow obtained a bottle of champagne. Knowing that the room was bugged he said to his companion in a clear voice how sorry he was that the person listening in to their conversation could not share in this 'delicious bottle of champagne'. About ten minutes later his room telephone rang. He lifted the receiver and the only sound he heard was the popping of a champagne cork and laughter and the phone then went dead again.

This was a short trip and the official purpose was for the repair of the x-ray equipment in the hospital and we had no further reason to stay. When we arrived back at Heathrow Airport we decided to have a cup of coffee together before the engineer headed to Swindon and I headed home. As a sign of how tight the security had been we were both sitting there continually looking over our shoulders before we realised we were back in the UK and no longer under surveillance. This was in September 1989.

It was just a few short months to Christmas and the events that unfolded over that season were astonishing. I was at my parents' home and listened to the hourly reports that were coming in about the downfall of Nicolae Ceausescu. It was quite strange to see the buildings that I had been walking around a few months earlier being hit by mortar fire. The fighting seemed severe. The events being recorded were perhaps the best Christmas present that one could have asked for, and especially for the poor people of Romania. The Ceausescu's were captured and with no hint of a trial were summarily executed. In the heyday of their rule I believe they sincerely thought that the crowds before them were there in adoration. The bewilderment on their faces as the crowd turned against them was clear to see. They were confused and perplexed. They could not understand why the people who 'loved them so dearly' were now so hostile. When you speak a lie so many times eventually you come to believe it.

I had the opportunity to return to Romania several times. On my second visit I met Pastor Petru Dugulescu in Timisoara. I learned from him what had happened on that Christmas season in his town. He had been used quite dramatically during the events that unfolded. As events further unravelled and democratic elections were held he became the member of Parliament for Timisoara. The last time I spoke to him he related that he had won eight other politicians for Christ in that time. I had the privilege of interviewing him about the events of that Christmas season and this is a précis his story…

"We heard that the tanks had been sent by Ceausescu and we were expecting serious troubles as they surrounded our town of Timisoara. In fact, news began to spread through the town that a miracle had taken place. The tanks which were sent against us to threaten us had turned around and were effectively protecting the town. Consequently, a large gathering built up in the massive square in the centre of the town and many speeches were made by the officials of the town. One of them suggested that as this was Christmas Eve there should be someone to speak for God. I knew instantly that I was to be that man and I went to the platform. I was not aware of what was happening in Bucharest but felt compelled to speak to the crowd about the truth of the gospel and the meaning of Christmas. When I had finished I said to the crowd that many of them had probably never prayed nor knew how to pray but perhaps some may remember 'The Lord's Prayer'. To my amazement and without being asked, this vast crowd sank to their knees and I led them in prayer. It was a most holy meeting."

Now that the Ceausescu's were dead, people from the West now had opportunity to visit Romania freely and were appalled by the poor conditions that they met. Those living in the rural areas were struggling harshly to feed themselves and their families. The compassion Westerners had for the children in the orphanages has, I believe, been well documented. Being free to travel I visited several villages and was humbled by the poverty and struggle for life experienced in these rural areas. As is the case in most situations where a dictator rules, the 'ruling class' lives in luxury and the poor people under there rule are left in dire situations.

Internal flights in Romania were an experience in themselves. The only airline, which was actually owned by the government, was called TAROM. I remember one flight which was particularly dire. I was flying from Bucharest to Timisoara and was duly settled in my window seat. As we took off the people in the front row were given what I assumed to be a glass of vodka. I assume this was the equivalent of first-class travel! For the rest of us poor people in the economy we were offered a sugar-coated candy and nothing else. This turned out to be nothing more than bubble-gum and it was only after this realisation that I noticed how many old and chewed pieces of gum had been stuck in various places inside the plane! As I was looking out of the window I saw beneath us an airport. I am not sure what our height was but in the back of my mind I believe it was at about 10,000 feet. I did not realise that this was Timisoara airport until the plane suddenly banked right and descended at great speed to the airport. Thankfully we landed safely but not too smoothly. I am sure that the airline has improved greatly. (I have to say that as I do not wish to be sued!)

As I write I am reminded of the flights into Tegucigalpa, the capital of Honduras which I visited on three occasions. The name of the air company was TACA which I understand was nicknamed 'Take A Chance Airway' by the locals. It is reckoned to be one of the most dangerous landings as aircraft have to come in over mountains and into a valley quite steeply. It is strange when making the final approach to the airport to look out of the window and be at the level of people's homes. But I digress.

The story of Lawrenciu was particularly sad. Brian had heard of this lad who lived with his family in the town of Suceava. He had a life-threatening heart condition and was in need of an urgent operation. Through the Protekon Trust, Brian had arranged for a top surgeon to perform the necessary surgery free of charge. The Trust would provide for other needs. Permission was needed for the boy to travel and I went to Suceava to speak with the parents, to explain the need and dangers of the operation and obtain his parents' permission. It was agreed Lawrenciu and his father would come to the UK for the operation. It was risky surgery and although he received the best of treatment sadly he did not pull through. His death affected us all quite deeply.

If the circumstances in Romania seemed difficult, the poverty experienced by the people in Albania made the former seem like a holiday camp! I again went there on behalf of the Protekton Trust to consider the viability of placing an x-ray machine in the hospital in the town of Sarande. The easiest way into Sarande was from Corfu. There was a small ferryboat (launch) with its fair share of the security men which left daily. Mike and Maggie, missionaries from Australia, were my first contact. When I visited the hospital with Mike I was almost physically sick. I believe I saw the worst possible medical conditions that I have witnessed anywhere in the world, including rural Africa. I can think of no word appalling enough to describe what I saw. It was squalid, begrimed, putrid. In the hospital grounds the medical waste, including used dressings and needles et cetera were just strewn around the ground. There were no containers for such dangerous waste and pigs were snuffling through it for food. I certainly did not eat pork on that visit!

Inside the hospital there were very few staff and they seemed totally demoralised. In the maternity unit, there appeared to be only one shower fitting which was presumably not working. The shower tray contained human faeces. It appeared that no one had been employed to clean any part of the hospital. It was repulsive. The table in the operating theatre was covered in thick dust. How a surgeon with any medical knowledge would want to even touch the facilities, let alone operate on them, was beyond my reasoning.

Outside in the yard was a fairly modern mobile ambulance which had been fully equipped and donated by another charity. It was standing idle and neglected since no one had been trained with the skills to either drive it or use the medical facilities. Additionally, there was no money to operate it even if medical staff and technicians were available. I have heard of similar situations. An appeal is made, sometimes even on children's television, to raise funds for a particular project and often for a piece of capital expenditure but no provision is made for the ongoing costs et cetera. Unless suitable provision is made then quite frankly it is a complete waste of money. It might make the presenters feel good but in practical terms many such efforts are futile. Mike did discuss with the technical personnel about the power input needed to power an x-ray machine but I believe that given all that we had seen it was not a difficult decision not to give this equipment.

The dictator Enva Hoxha, who died in 1985, had told his people that the people of Albania were so rich and the people of the surrounding nations in Europe were so poor that it was necessary for the safety and well-being of the citizens to close the borders so tightly. As a result of the lie that he sold to his people the whole countryside was littered with what I can only describe as concrete mushrooms. They had been placed as shelters for the people to use in the event of an air attack from a hostile nation. They were so badly constructed that they would have been totally inadequate and not able to give one iota of protection. Even had a large bird landed on them I suspect some of them would have toppled over!

Mike and Maggie were working hard in in extremely difficult circumstances as missionaries. There was one church in Sarande planted out from a church on Corfu but they were suspicious about working with the missionary family. In general, food supplies in this communist regime were far from plentiful and somewhat expensive. On one occasion I accompanied Mike over a small rocky mountain to a village where he was hoping to see the start of a new church. He had been working in the village for some time and there were a few believers who we visited in their homes. It is strange that when people are living in such poverty that somehow they manage to find the means to produce alcohol. In Albania their drink was called raki and it was a very potent and raw spirit. They had little to offer us in hospitality and raki seemed the only thing on offer! Some, who have not been involved in cross-cultural mission would have rebuked us for accepting this hospitality but the offence of refusing may have done more harm than good in leading these people to the Lord. I accepted a small thimble size amount but after visiting the third home, I said to Mike we should stop evangelising for the day. I was not sure I would make it safely back over the rocks!

There have been many times when I have been offered food and drink that I most certainly would not, in normal circumstances consume. In Cameroon, for example, on my last day in Douala, the pastor's daughter said she had cooked a real delicacy for me for my final supper. When the food was served I thought that it would literally be my 'last supper' as it turned out to be a snail stew. These were not the nice sanitised garlic covered escargot but snails of various sizes collected from the forest! I tried to look as delighted as she was as I somehow managed to eat the over large dish and extremely over large snails that were put before me!

As with Romania, communism in Albania eventually fell. There was a great deal of anger felt by the citizens when they realised how they had been deceived, oppressed and lied to. Much to their own loss the citizens of Sarande went on the rampage. They wanted to destroy anything that had belonged to the government. It was not safe to be in the town at that time. They released the prisoners from jail and even took control of a gunship which they subsequently used to fire back onto the town! It was only when their anger subsided that they realised that the government had effectively owned everything, and they had destroyed most of the basic infrastructure of the town.

I visited Sarande on several occasions but when Mike and Maggie decided to leave with their young family my visits stopped.

Chapter 6

Stoned!

I have always had a love for Israel. I understand that it is a secular nation and that at times the political decisions that it makes do not seem the wisest but they are the only true democracy in the Middle East. About 20% of the population is Arab and they have full representation in the Israeli parliament, the Knesset. This in contrast to its Middle Eastern neighbours who for the most part wish to see the destruction of this tiny country. I believe the covenant promise that God gave the land to the descendants of Abraham, Isaac and Jacob was an everlasting covenant and that covenant still stands. The fact that the Jewish people have survived the Diaspora (the dispersion or spread of any people from their original homeland) for some 2000 years and yet kept their identity until their nation was reborn in 1948 is testimony that God is a covenant keeping God. Indeed, the rebirth of this tiny nation is, to my mind, a modern miracle.

The fact that our God is a covenant keeping God is fundamental to understanding how to live a life of faith. If God were fickle how could we depend on Him? If we could not depend on Him how could we trust His promises and if we could not trust His promises where is the basis for our faith – it becomes only hope. It is because there is no shadow of turning with Him that our faith has a foundation.

Over the years I have found it much easier to pray when walking. I am fortunate that I can often go along by the river or to my beloved Greenwich Park. One Saturday morning I was in the park praying and I distinctly remember saying to the Lord, *"You know that I would love to visit Israel. If I do not hear from you about this by the end of today, I will stop asking."* I forgot this prayer until about 9pm that evening. I did not know Bruce very well in those days, but he phoned me and said, *"I believe that God wants you to go to Israel and I will pay for your fare!"* As you can imagine it did not take me long to concur and about two months later I was on an El

Al plane bound for Tel Aviv with another dear friend, Rob. He was going to visit Pastor Ted (no not Father Ted!). This was the first in a journey of many miracles that we experienced on our visit.

Why do I tell so many stories of miracles and healings et cetera? Because God is unchanging. The Bible says, '*He is the same yesterday today and for ever*'. In these days so much of the spiritual power of the church has been lost. I do not mean the temporal power as exemplified by the Catholic church. The church and individual Christians are a supernatural people with a commission to bring the Kingdom of God down to the earth. When we are living in the same supernatural power that God poured out at Pentecost we too will see the miracle working power of God. What God did for the Old Testament saints, what he did through Jesus and what he did through the apostles, he still does today.

Christianity is much more about faith than it is about belief. It is possible to believe anything if you choose to. You can choose to believe that black is white or that the earth is flat! Believing this is only the first step. Faith starts with the person and nature of God. If we believe who He is and that His Word is truth, then faith rests in the knowledge that He is not double-minded and will do what He has promised. Gods' response may not always be immediate but we consider that we have the answer before it is given. Putting this trust in His promises into action enables God to fulfil His promise. The Bible describes faith in this way: "*Faith is the substance of things hoped for, the evidence of things not seen.*" Faith comprehends as fact what has not yet been experienced by the physical senses.

My main purpose in writing this book goes beyond just the recounting of anecdotes et cetera. My hope is that by reading the experiences of an ordinary man walking with an extraordinary God you will be encouraged in your understanding that God is unchanging. If you believe and act on His promises you too can see the power of God in your life. I recall a young evangelist saying to me, "*It's okay for you Stan. You go to all these places where God is moving. But it doesn't happen here!*" I was somewhat taken

59

aback. Believe me, it does happen here if we step out in faith, trusting in the promises of God. I asked him when he had last prayed for someone who was sick. He looked somewhat sheepish and said it had been several years. No wonder he was not seeing the fulfilment of God's power in his life and in the lives of those around him.

If we are not prepared to step out in faith and trust that what the Lord says, the Lord will do, we will not see Him moving in our own lives. Over the years I have witnessed most of the miracles that were seen by the New Testament saints, simply because I choose to believe that God is faithful to his word. Indeed, one of my favourite hymns is 'Great is Thy Faithfulness'.

> *Great is thy faithfulness, oh God my father.*
> *There is no shadow of turning with thee.*
> *Thou changest not - thy compassions they fail not.*
> *As thou hast been thou forever shall be.*

And the chorus…

> *Great is thy faithfulness! Great is thy faithfulness!*
> *Morning by morning new mercies I see.*
> *All I have needed thy hand hath provided.*
> *Great is thy faithfulness, Lord, unto me.*

Neither Rob nor myself had much money when we arrived at Tel Aviv airport. While we were waiting for our baggage we saw many advertisements for car hire and we remarked what a shame it was that we could not afford to rent a car to travel more freely. We were being met by a friend that Rob had met on an earlier visit. After greeting us he told us that he had some spare cash and the Lord had told him in a dream to give it to us to rent a car! This we did with no hesitation and we soon found ourselves heading north to Galilee and Mount Carmel. Elijah, the prophet of fire, has always been my favourite Old Testament prophet. I was thrilled to go to the site where the defeat of the prophets of Baal took place.

We stayed at a nearby retreat run by Messianic Jews and on our second evening ate at a restaurant in the Druze village of Isfiya. Having eaten, Yusuf, the restaurant owner, invited us into his home. This must have been a 'God thing' as we had only had a short conversation with him up to this point as he served our food. We later discovered that he was one of the leaders of the Druze people. It was fascinating to hear from him what the Druze people believe. They are an Abrahamic religion who revere Jethro, the father-in-law of Moses. He is their spiritual founder and chief prophet. We also had opportunity to share with Yusuf and his family what we believed as Christians. He agreed for me to send him a copy of the New Testament in his own language when we got home.

We continued north to Metula. This is a town at the northern end of Israel on the border of Lebanon. We stayed with an American mission family. This was not the easiest town to stay in. I understood many of the homes had built-in bunkers for protection when rockets came from the North. We could see tanks rolling through the meandering hills in the security belt between the two countries. Their sound rattled our beds as they patrolled through the night. The Good Fence was a border crossing from Metula to Lebanon opened in 1976 and subsequently closed in 2000 after Israel's withdrawal from Lebanon. The border crossing allowed the population of southern Lebanon to find jobs in northern Israel, have access to health services, attend school in Israel and transport goods. It also allowed Christians from Lebanon to cross into Israel to join in the services of a small church. We were privileged to attend a meeting in that church.

I have always loved the sound of the shofar (rams' horn). It was my joy to be able to stand at this northern tip of Israel, facing south, and blow the shofar, as it had been blown throughout the land in the times of the Bible. I was thankful for my days in the Boys Brigade bugle band that enabled me to make a respectable sound!

Many people told me that I would probably not enjoy my visit to Israel because all the biblical sites have been covered by religious buildings. I am not a religious man. I find religion is a way for men to control Christianity. I believe that true Christianity is about a relationship with the Living God through His son Jesus Christ. Just as I had a natural relationship with my earthly father so I have a supernatural relationship with my heavenly Father.

Rob and I determined from the beginning that we would not be deterred by the man-made religious monuments and shrines nor be in or awe of their splendour. There is no doubt that many of them are fine buildings. Instead, we chose to sit outside with our open Bibles and read the passages relevant to the places we were visiting. In this respect, one of the most moving experiences was to stand at the front of the ruins of the synagogue at Capernaum and perhaps stand at the very place that Jesus stood. I read aloud the very Scripture that Jesus himself read at the beginning of His ministry. (Although He did not read it at this site). *"The Spirit of the Lord is upon me, because he has anointed me to preach the good news to the poor; he has sent me to heal the broken-hearted, to proclaim liberty to the captives and recovery of sight to the blind, to set at liberty those who are oppressed; to proclaim the acceptable year of the Lord."* A tingle ran down my spine as I repeated these words from the Prophet Isaiah and a tingle still runs down my spine when I read them today.

We visited many of the biblical sites in the country north of Jerusalem and I have wonderful memories of all that the Lord showed us through that visit. To sit by the statue of Elijah on Mount Carmel and read the story I mentioned above; to sit on the shores of the Sea of Galilee and read the sermon on the Mount; to climb the hill of transfiguration where Jesus was seen with Moses and Elijah transfigured in all His glory; to rest by the River Jordan, perhaps at the site where Jesus himself was baptised. To read the relevant Bible passages at these sites was exhilarating and brought to life the wonderful stories.

At the ruins of Megiddo I stood looking across the Plain of Jezreel. This is the site of the soon to come Battle of Armageddon. I am not sure if this is still the situation but it was noticeable that there was virtually no property built on this plain. I am not one given very frequently to visions but as I stood there I had a vision of the Second Coming of Jesus! It was as real as if it was unfolding before my very eyes. I saw an immense battle raging and filling the whole of that mighty plain. It appeared to me as a very conventional battle with shells and mortars and the like being fired. It did not look a very ordered battle but there was quite a melee. It was amazing, awesome and somewhat frightening. Suddenly, as I watched I heard the sounding of a mighty trumpet (shofar) and I looked up and to my right coming through the sky in all His glory was the Lord Jesus, King of Kings and Lord of Lords. At the sounding of the shofar the fighting somehow instantly died down. Although it was very noisy as the battle raged every ear heard the sound. The Lord was descending in all his splendour and majesty and followed by his vast army of saints as prophesied in the Book of Revelation. They were descending towards the battleground. It was a captivating and breath-taking moment. Rob, not knowing what I was seeing, nudged me and said, *"Come along Stan, it's time to move on"*. I would have loved to have stayed longer and seen the unfolding of this event but the vision ended and it was not to be. The remembrance of the vision has remained with me very strongly. When I returned home I realised the Lord had imparted to me a clear understanding of the biblical situation concerning the nation of Israel, the church and the 'last days' that I did not have before seeing this vision. I have attempted to write some of this understanding in my book, *"Are We There Yet?"*

Our journey continued through the northern parts of Israel and we found ourselves following a road on the Golan Heights. This is a particularly sensitive area and it is understandable why the Heights are so controversial and so important to the security of Israel. From here it is possible to see across a large part of the tiny nation. I was still using a 35mm camera in those and not a modern digital version and so from time to time I needed to change the film. It was here that I needed a new film and my camera being old, I wanted to be sure that light did not get into the film. I put a sleeping bag over my head and proceeded to fumble in the dark to change the film. Whilst inside the sleeping bag and unknown to me an Israeli security patrol had approached and asked Rob what I was doing. Rob told them, *"Don't worry, he is English!"* As if that would explain everything! I am not sure how Rob expected this to satisfy them but I think he wanted to allay their fears that nothing untoward was happening. I finally extricated myself with film and camera in hand and explained to their satisfaction.

It turned out that this was not the reason they had been curious about our presence there. Where we had stopped we were alongside a fenced field behind which were some beautiful wild flowers. I had gone through the barbed wire to gather some. Unbeknown to me, until they enlightened me, the field I had wandered in was part of the buffer zone between Syria and Israel and in addition to being full of beautiful flowers it was also full of not so beautiful mines! I am so pleased that God gives His angels charge over us in all our stupid ways. *'Even though I walk through the valley of the shadow of death, I will fear no evil, for you are with me.'* Surely, God is faithful to every one of his promises.

Our excitement on this day was not over nor had we seen the worst of our troubles. In Israel, vehicles registered to Israelis have a yellow number plate and those registered to the Palestinians are blue. Having hired our little Fiat Uno at Tel Aviv airport we were driving with yellow number plates. On that particular Friday afternoon, we had an amazing deliverance from danger. Some ten days previously an event happened that the newspapers had called the 'Hebron Massacre'. An Israeli had gone berserk and killed many Palestinians. The Guardian newspaper reported that in all at least 55 people were killed, and scores wounded. It was the biggest peacetime death toll since the Jewish state was founded in 1948. The Hebron massacre was the work of a single man, Baruch Goldstein.

Friday being the day when Muslims attend the mosque, tensions were running high. Because of the massacre the messages from the mosques that day were extremely violent towards all Israelis, more so than usual. Rob and I were heading back to Jerusalem to leave our bags with Pastor Ted before returning the car to Tel Aviv airport. Somehow we got onto the wrong road and instead of travelling on the safe Israeli road we found ourselves travelling through the West Bank! In normal circumstances this would not have presented too much of a problem but on this day, after the Mosques had emptied, the circumstances were far from normal.

Unaware of our mistake we were happily bouncing along towards Nablus in our little Fiat Uno, totally oblivious to the trouble ahead. We were simply enjoying a pleasant afternoon drive. As we rounded a bend in the road we saw a line of rocks blocking our passage. Suddenly, what sounded like gunfire was all around us. I genuinely thought we were being shot at. Mobile phones do of course have their uses but on this day, it turned out that the Palestinians in Nablus had been made aware that this 'Israeli' car was heading their way. Just outside of the town they were waiting for us. As we stopped because of the row of rocks we realised that they had set up a trap for us by a small cliff. The rocks across the road were to force us to stop. What we thought was gunfire was the sound of rocks showering down on us and hitting the car. Both Rob and I went into prayer mode. Rob was obviously more spiritual than I! He was praying for angelic protection. On the other hand, because I had a $200 deposit for the car against my credit card which I could ill afford I was praying for protection for the car as I did not wish to lose this money! I managed to manoeuvre around the roadblock and as we rounded the next corner to our great relief there was an Israeli army checkpoint.

"What are you doing here?" one of the soldiers bellowed. *"You can't come through this way. The town is under curfew." "Well we certainly can't go back!"* I replied and explained what had happened just behind us. Following the preaching at the mosque that morning the residents of town had been rioting and therefore the whole town had been placed under curfew by the soldiers. They agreed to escort us through Nablus. Eight of them climbed on to their personnel carrier with their guns pointing at the homes and rooftops as we passed through the main street. *"Stay as close to us as you can and whatever you do don't stop,"* was the instruction as they

took off at great speed with me in my little Fiat Uno nose to tail behind them as the Palestinians were showering all sorts of things down upon us from the high buildings on either side.

We got through safely and the soldiers dismounted from their vehicle at the other end of the town and we got out of our little Fiat. They just looked at us and the little car with amazement. In spite of many rocks having hit the vehicle there was neither dent nor scratch to be found anywhere on the whole of the bodywork nor were any windows broken. It seemed that the Lord had answered both of our prayers. Angels to protect us and to bat away the rocks and to save my $200 deposit! Before we left, we had opportunity to talk to these wonderful young men about the Lord Jesus.

As if we had not had enough troubles that day, we ended up with a puncture going through Ramallah. We were still in the West Bank and obviously not completely clear of danger as immediately two Israeli soldiers came and stood by us for protection as we put on the spare wheel. We were driving on to Tel Aviv airport to return the car when the heavens opened, and a torrential downpour washed the car clean of any possible residual evidence of our experience. *'He will give his angels charge over you, lest you dash your foot against a stone.'* Yet another example of the faithfulness of the Lord and the trustworthiness of His word, the Bible. I do not want to go anywhere without His presence.

We had no idea where we would be staying back in Jerusalem for the second week. Having returned the car to Tel Aviv airport we took the bus back to Jerusalem. We went first to visit pastor Ted who, with his wife, was staying at the home of Tamara, a beautiful Jewish Christian believer. I took to her straightaway when she asked, *'Where are you boys staying?'* We told her we had not yet worked that out and she informed us that she had an apartment in her basement which was empty for just that week and we were able to stay there without payment. This was right in the centre of Jerusalem and covered our accommodation costs for the second week. In addition, she cooked a meal for us every evening and it was a joy on the Friday before we flew home to share a Shabbat meal with her. This meal had been made really special. An Arab neighbour had brought some unleavened bread for our Shabbat and we were also joined by Boris, a Russian Jew who had recently moved to Jerusalem and had also met with his Messiah, Jesus Christ. The Shabbat is a shared meal which starts the beginning of the Jewish Sabbath or day of rest. It is only in the love of Jesus Christ that Jew and Arab, English and Russian are able to live in true peace.

I do not recall that we got into any further troubles in the second week but again visited many of the biblical sites in this wonderful and beautiful city. It seems strange that my favourite place and my least favourite place are both about the burial of Jesus. The Tomb of the Holy Sepulchre felt to me like one of the most spiritually dark places that I had ever entered. To me it bore no spiritual resemblance to the biblical account of the kind of tomb in which Jesus would have been laid. There is constant arguing between the various Christian sects to whom control has been given. Whether or not this unlikely place is that of the Lord's burial I have my doubts. Regardless, they do Christianity a great disservice by their actions. As we descended into the darkness of this place I asked Rob what Jesus would think today if He came to this place. His immediate reply made me smile, *"He would not come in here!"*

By contrast, the Garden Tomb across a busy road and adjacent to the Arab bus station is a place of immense peace in the bustle of such a busy city. No claim is made that this tomb is the actual burial place but it is almost adjacent to Golgotha where the Lord was crucified. The tomb itself is carved from rock and has a circular stone that could easily be rolled in front of the entrance. To me, it did not matter whether this was the actual tomb. What did matter was the beautiful peace in the garden that enabled reflection and prayer. It is certainly my favourite place in all of Israel.

We visited many other wonderful places in Jerusalem and I returned on two other occasions to Israel, but the telling fits better into other parts of this book.

Chapter 7

God Meant It for Good

Way back in the Bible, the book of Genesis tells the story of Joseph. Joseph is the youngest of 12 brothers and his father favours him to such an extent that his brothers hate him to the point that they wish to kill him. He receives a clear dream concerning his future. He boasts about this dream to his brothers who hate him even more. They sell him into slavery. He later finds himself betrayed by the wife of the household into which he is brought and finds himself in prison. Telling a long story in a few sentences, after a series of dreams, he is raised up to such high position in Egypt that during a famine his brothers come begging for food which has been stored by Joseph in Egypt. When the brothers, who had sold him into slavery, recognise it is their young brother to whom they bow down they are terrified, thinking that now Joseph will take his revenge upon them. However, the difficult circumstances through which Joseph had come have made him the man God wanted him to be. Instead of taking revenge he tells his brothers, "*You meant your actions for harm, but God meant it for good!*"

Dreams from God are not confined to characters in the Bible. The prophet Joel said '*in the last days young men will have visions and old men dream dreams*' I have moved into stage two! We should never limit God. Not so long ago I had a bad fall on the pavement. Among several injuries was my knee. I could not kneel on it without an excruciating pain. In a dream I was at a meeting and went forward for prayer for healing for my knee. When I awoke my knee was completely pain free and continues to be so.

Through the years, God has often asked me to do difficult things or has asked me difficult questions. One such question that took me about three weeks before I could answer in the affirmative was simply, "*if I wish to use you as a martyr, do I have your permission?*" He did not say that he would use me in such a way but needed to know if I were so submitted that if he chose to he could do so. I believe that my positive reply has enabled me to travel into areas that others have feared to go.

On another occasion he asked, *"Do I have your permission to break you?"* One common thread is that the Holy Spirit is a gentleman and was asking my permission rather than telling me that these things would happen. I asked him further what this would entail and whilst he did not fill in the detail, so to speak, suggested that the loss of the fellowship that I was pastoring at that time or the loss of my reputation might be consequences. It took a while to come through with a positive answer with both of these questions. Now having experienced two betrayals, both of which nearly broke me, I was beginning to understand more what it was like to be fully submitted to the Lord.

I have, in an earlier chapter, talked about how I felt betrayed at the time of stepping down from the ministry of Pastor. It is neither fruitful nor beneficial to write about the circumstances. I only mention it to say that what happened was a steppingstone to a widening of my ministry as I started to travel abroad. After some years working in Kenya a situation arose that once again left me feeling betrayed. As before, I will not recount the circumstances, but I know that both of these 'betrayals' left me heartbroken. However, they were a catalyst to open many new opportunities not just in Kenya but very widely in Africa. In both 'betrayals' I have found reconciliation and with hindsight can also see that as painful as these happenings were at the time, God has used them for good. God speaks to me often through rainbows, and even in this second betrayal God gave me a personal miracle. I was sitting heartbroken in the Kenyan sunshine with a clear blue, cloudless sky. I simply said to the Lord with tear-filled eyes, *"I need a rainbow!"* In a moment, under circumstances where it would be thought of as impossible, a beautiful perfectly formed rainbow appeared in the sky and lasted for about fifteen minutes. The comfort this rainbow gave me carried me through. I will write more about miracles in a later chapter.

When you live in dependence on the Lord and upon his promises you never lack provision. There is what I call a false teaching that some call 'the prosperity doctrine'. Basically, it says that God wants you rich. If you are not rich you are not living in the blessings of God. I even heard a preacher in Africa tell a large crowd of leaders that if a man is not rich then he will not have him to speak in his church! I was furious and tried to speak with him after the meeting but he jumped into his massive four-wheel-drive vehicle and drove away before I could reach him. Such teaching suggests that he would not have allowed Jesus Himself into his pulpit since by his definition Jesus was not prospering because he had no material wealth! I was reminded of the occasion when Jesus needed money to pay the Temple Tax in Jerusalem. It is clear He had no money nor personal riches. He sent Peter to fish and Peter miraculously found a coin in the fish's mouth. Again, in His teaching, Jesus said, *"The Son of Man has nowhere to lay his head."* By the definition of the 'so-called' prosperity doctrine, Jesus himself did not prosper! Ridiculous and offensive!

Why offensive? Many of the congregation were rural pastors who had almost nothing in material terms. Many of them had probably walked many miles to listen to this preacher, and how condemned they must have felt at the evangelists' teaching. They had, for the most part, small congregations who could barely support themselves let alone a pastor. Yet these men certainly knew what it was to live by faith, and working with many of them, I learnt a great deal from them.

Initially, after the second betrayal, I did stop working with George but we did reconcile again in later years and I am happy to say that his son, Eric, has learned from the mistakes that his father made. Now The Lords Ministry has grown beautifully. I still had sufficient funds to enable me to return to Kenya, so I decided to make what I thought would be a final trip to Africa. I had only been working with George up to this point. I had made many friends in my earlier travels and decided to accept some of the invitations which many of these wonderful men had given me. In the rural areas of Kenya there are so many men working hard and sacrificially for the kingdom of God.

One such man was Mike W. On my first visit to Kenya I travelled to Namanjalala, and in the home of Pastor Vitalis held a day of seminars for a small group of leaders. It is a very remote area almost unreachable except on foot when the rains come. My subject was unity and young Pastor Mike was sitting wide-eyed listening to this visiting mzungu (white man). I lost touch with him for several years until one day in Kitale town we were reunited. Unbeknown to me the message of unity had struck a solid chord in his heart. He had consequently started a new ministry, IGEM, which has worked to unite many ministries and churches not only across Kenya but in many other African nations. I have had the privilege to travel with him on many occasions and hold unity conferences with him. I know that around Africa there are over 1000 ministries signed up to IGEM. As an itinerant missionary I do not always realise how far or how effective a word can reach. From one small meeting in one small village and one young pastor, has grown an extremely large unifying organisation. A great ministry from such a small seed.

It has been said that the growth of Christianity in sub Saharan Africa is like an extremely broad river flowing across the continent but lacking in depth. People are receiving Jesus in large numbers but are not being well taught. Whilst I love open-air meetings and what we call 'crusade meetings' I was seeing more and more that there was a need for solid biblical teaching. I would never turn away an invitation to preach the gospel open-air but my heart was growing to see these rural pastors being better trained. I began holding many seminars and conferences for church leaders. I would often hold a question and answer session during these meetings. I was amazed at the simplicity and lack of understanding of basic biblical principles these dear pastors had. I developed a basic teaching course which I called 'Firm Foundations'. It was a privilege to be able to teach many groups of leaders in the foundational truths of the faith that they so clearly possessed. I subsequently put the teachings into a series of twelve booklets that could be used as a self-teaching resource or for use in small group meetings. It is still available in digital form and I understand it has been used in many other situations including in a jail in the United States.

Another observation of the church, not just in Africa, but across the world is a profound lack of unity. I found that teaching unity became quite central to much of my teaching. So much so that I consolidated my teaching into a new book simply entitled '*Unity*' with a subtitle '*Wholeness for the Church*'. In Africa disunity reached such epic proportions that even the Kenyan Government at one time recognised that there were simply too many applications for the registration of new churches and ministries. At one time they had stopped issuing new registrations. I was told by one potential ministry leader that he was watching a struggling ministry and was praying that it would fail so that he might take up his registration. You may imagine that my response was not one of blessing!

As my work in Africa expanded I was delighted to meet Simon Changorok. He has gone now to be with the Lord but he was one of the most joyful men I have ever met. I said of him he had only ever laughed once in his life. His laugh started when he was born and he has not stopped laughing since. Of course, like all of us he has had his struggles, but his joy was infectious. He was of the Pokot tribe. He was held in great respect not only among his own people but among the neighbouring people of Turkana, Marakwet, and Karamoja. He too had a vision for unity and together we developed a strategy of holding unity conferences with open-air crusade meetings. The leaders who attended the conference would then work together in an open-air meeting. This outward demonstration of their unity at the meetings brought great blessing. Testimonies came through that as they worked together in unity, they began to see great success. Many hundreds came to put their trust in Jesus and we received many testimonies of healing. It was not unusual to hear from a pastor that his harvest, both physical and spiritual increased dramatically following the conferences.

Politicians will often attend these meetings, not always in support but looking for opportunities to make speeches. I resisted this as much as possible although when they came I always welcomed them and gave them due honour. In one town it had been reported that a local councillor, Lucy, had been persecuting the churches and had even demolished the Catholic church. I did not speak nor understand the language of the Pokot people so when I saw this lady on the crusade platform speaking with great gusto I was uncertain as to what was happening. It transpired that this was the same Lucy who had been persecuting the churches. She had been at the meeting on the previous day. This time it was not a political speech but she was declaring that she had received Jesus, telling the people that now when they visit her home they will no longer be given alcohol but soda! To us it was a sign of the blessings of the unity promised in Psalm 133. When we were in Makutano, Lucy would often join us.

One young girl of about 11 years old came to me at the end of the meeting. She was in tears as she had recently lost both her parents and was being cared for by her aunt. She asked if we could help with her education and I was so moved by her plea that I kept in touch with her and paid her education for about three years. What happened after this was utterly amazing and when I met her more than 10 years later she confirmed the story.

President Moi was holding a political rally at Makutano Stadium. Young Harriet felt moved by the Holy Spirit and fasted for three days before the president came. On that day she was part of a dance group that was to perform and so it was fairly easy for her to have access to the VIP platform. It was an extremely dangerous thing for her to do. She had written a short letter to the president and at great risk, certainly of arrest and possibly of being shot, she approached the platform and knelt before the president. His security rushed to move her away but he stopped them and bade her approach. The letter was asking him to help with her future education. He was so moved, not only referring to her in his speech, but agreeing to take her into his sponsored school which gives one of the best educations for girls in the whole of Kenya. He paid for her uniform and books et cetera even to the point of sending one of his official limousines to collect her and take her to the first day at school. How young Harriet reminded us of Queen Esther who approached King Artaxerxes with the words, *"If I perish, I perish!"* Miracles still happen if we believe!

Two streets away was my favourite restaurant in that area. It was run by Somalis and the best item on the menu was 'boiled meat'. This consisted of a leg of goat, a sharp knife, and a plate of ugali with sukuma wiki. (basically maize flower made into a paste and served with boiled kale!). It may not sound that exciting, but that goat meat was delicious. After one crusade, we went back to their restaurant for goat. We were excited when they told us that although they could not hear the meeting from their restaurant they knew when we were preaching because they found themselves shaking. We had the privilege of praying for them. After that, every time we returned, they would ask us for prayer and give us a private room to eat our boiled meat feast.

The weather in western Kenya is often fairly predictable. At certain times of year there is a heavy afternoon shower. Not a gentle British shower that we would know but an African downpour that may produce a couple of inches of rain in an hour. On the first day of a three-day meeting this huge downpour caused our meeting to be abandoned. As we were setting up for the second day, we could see these large clouds

74

gathering. We were on the side of Mount Elgon and the horizon was dozens of miles beyond. These rain clouds appeared and were coming towards us. I asked Simon whether the people to the west in Kolongolo or to the east in Uasin Gishu were more in need of the blessing of rain. He said the people to the west and so we commanded that rain to go to Kolongolo. It was awesome to see the storm change direction and leave us unhampered by the weather. So as to show no favours we sent it to Uasin Gishu the next day! I really did miss working with Simon when he passed away.

Another man that I worked with at this time was Bishop Robert. He had established churches across East Africa and invited me to accompany him on a visit to Goma in the Democratic Republic of the Congo. Three things made this probably the most difficult journey that I made in all my time in Africa. Firstly, we were to travel on African roads with African transport. Secondly there was always the danger of civil war and Goma was physically the most inhospitable town in which to live. Thirdly, although I did not realise when we set out, I was about to display the symptoms of another malarial attack. What a journey! I found my old travel diary for that journey and have copied it word for word. It was as bad as I remember it!

> **_Day One!_** *We left the Kitale at 8-30 on the first two-hour leg by matatu to Bungoma.* (A matatu is a privately owned minibus/taxi so-called because the fare always used to be three shillings - in Swahili the word for three is tatu.) *A poor second leg on a very crowded matatu to Malaba, the border crossing to Uganda. The only problem at the border was the heat! A good but long third leg to Kampala arriving at about 5-30pm. We missed our contact so we settled for two very seedy rooms in downtown Kampala. I think it is the local 'knocking-shop', but so far no one is knocking at my door!* (Yes! I have spent the night with a bishop in a brothel!) *Tomorrow we stay in Kampala and see if we can find the Congolese embassy and reassess our plans. What will tomorrow bring?*

> **_Day Two!_** *Survived the night. The last I heard before sleeping was the music in the bar at 12-55am! Managed to wash and shave etc. in about half a cup of water. We walked for ages to find a cup of tea and something to eat - our hotel does not provide such luxuries! (No complaints - it was*

better than the street - just!) No trouble at the bank where I was able to get more dollars in case of need and also Ugandan shillings. Taxi to the Embassy of the DRC (Democratic Republic of Congo). No trouble with visas at $50 each! We decided to set out and got a bus to Kabale, about a six-hour journey. It is set in a valley of rolling hills and is quite pretty if you don't look at the town. An excellent and very welcome chicken curry, a hot shower and bed.

Day Three! *Goma at last! But what a journey. Three days and each worse than the last. Today took just under twelve hours to cover 116 miles (an average of 9.8mph)! If there is a slow way of doing things, then these guys are the experts. First stop after one mile to change two tyres, then into a back street to fill up with black market petrol. Back to the street where we picked up two more passengers and argue about the cost of tyres. Off at last picking up a few more passengers as we went. En route there was a big and lengthy argument about the route to take. I believe we went the longer and steeper way, and because of the number of passengers we had to get out at the steeper parts and walk. Next a police check. After about an hour's delay two passengers were held by the police. During this delay the driver was able to re-secure the petrol tank, which had worked its way lose. After another hour the two are released again (after the exchange of money) and we are off, thankfully mainly downhill!*

At the next town we unload our bags as the driver said he would go no further. Having done so they changed their minds and we loaded up again. A free tour of the town (!) before we set off again and finally reached the border. No problems at either side of the border. The official on the Congolese side of the border was so keen to help everyone that he lost concentration on what he was doing and took about 45 minutes to stamp a visa that we already had!

We found a vehicle going to Goma and after a tour of another town set off for the town. The load on top of the vehicle did not like potholes and kept falling off. However, we eventually made it to Goma and had a two-mile walk to the hotel ------ but at last a hot shower, hot meal, hot tea and <u>cold</u> drinking water and bed."

One thing that my old travel diary does not mention was that throughout this trip I was suffering from malaria. I did not log it because I was unaware. I knew I was not well but just assumed I had taken some bad water. This certainly compounded the difficulties of such a potentially stressful journey.

I had been advised to carry a few packets of cigarettes with me. Not for personal consumption but to give to the security forces to smooth our passage if necessary. I must confess that I was more than a little nervous when confronted by a child soldier, a boy of no more than 13, who stopped us on the road. He was carrying an AK-47 rifle and seemed as nervous when he saw a Westerner as I was when I saw the child with such a dangerous weapon. I doubt he had ever seen a Westerner on this road before and was uncertain whether he should take any action. It was some time before he was satisfied that I was not a security threat and to be honest the cigarettes helped to convince him.

To my mind, Goma is probably one of the most difficult towns in which to live. It is built on a foundation of volcanic rock from the nearby volcano which is then covered with up to one inch of grey volcanic dust. A combination of humidity from nearby Lake Kivu, an equatorial sun from which the dust seems to hold the heat and the dust itself make for a very inhospitable environment. Not that I particularly cared by this time. However, I did my 'duty' in meeting the various church leaders and fulfilled all my preaching engagements but as soon as my responsibilities were finished I returned straight to my bed. Even at that time Goma was very insecure and contingency plans had been laid for a quick escape using the United Nations aircraft but these thankfully proved unnecessary. At night it was possible to see the glow of the volcano but it did not erupt whilst we were there. However, a few years later reports were in the international media that the volcano had indeed erupted again and pictures of the town being split in two by a lava flow were incredibly sad to see. I had no reports of the safety of the churches that I had visited but trust all was well with them.

Whether it was because we were moving away from a security area or not, the return journey, whilst being equally long, was comparatively incident free and after two days I arrived back happily in Kitale where I was able to take a beautiful hot shower. By now the malarial fever was abating and I was able to prepare for my return to Nairobi via Mount Kenya where I held another series of meetings before flying home.

These are certainly not the only wonderful men and women of God that I worked with through those years. They are to be honoured as they struggle in often difficult situations and with such limited resources. They are building new churches, supporting widows and orphans, providing healthcare, visiting the sick and those in prison. A complete book could not record the dedicated work of so many fine men and women.

Chapter 8

That Was a Miracle

Does God still work miracles today? For me there is no doubt. Any happening without a rational empirical explanation is to me a miracle. One of the best quotations that I have found that helps modern man to understand how miracles can happen comes from G K Chesterton. He wrote, *"If a man believes in unalterable natural law, he cannot believe in any miracle in any age. If a man believes in a will behind law, he can believe in any miracle in any age"*. In my simpler way I like to say that God created everything and set in motion the laws behind his creation. As the creator he has the ability, authority and power to set those laws apart in response to the faith of those who dare to believe. Was the restoration of Vitalis's maize a miracle? Yes, it was. Was flying from Nairobi to London without a ticket or money a miracle? Yes, it was. Was the diverting of a rainstorm from a meeting a miracle? Some may say it was a coincidence. This happened on three consecutive days and I class it as a miracle.

You see, the Bible says that the reason that Jesus came was to destroy all the work of the devil. The devil's work is to destroy as much of the work of God through His believers as he is able. When God created Adam He gave him authority (power; Gk: *dunamis- dynamite*) over His total creation. Before the fall of man (when Adam and Eve rebelled against God by eating the forbidden fruit) Adam had authority to represent God in every respect on the earth. This was to be passed down through the generations. When Adam and Eve rebelled much of the authority that God had given them was lost. On the cross Jesus cried with a loud voice, *"it is finished!"* He was not speaking about his life. He was saying that the work that he came to do, namely, to destroy the work of the devil, is finished - it is accomplished. The authority lost in Adam was restored and returned to believing men and women.

When Jesus returned to heaven, He said to the disciples who were with Him, *"All authority* (power; Gk: *dunamis- dynamite) in heaven and on earth is given to me. Therefore, you go into all the world and preach the good news."* The church, which is simply made up of all who believe in Jesus, have the authority (power; Gk: *dunamis- dynamite)* that was lost in Adam.

Whilst Jesus as the Son of God has always had the authority in heaven, when He came to this earth in the form of a man He always referred to Himself as the Son of Man. Because the sin of Adam and all men was in the flesh, He came as a fleshly man to destroy the sin of the flesh for all who believe in Him. The Bible puts it this way *'Since the children have flesh and blood, He too shared in their humanity so that by his death He might break the power of him who holds the power of death—that is, the devil'*

Jesus said that all authority in heaven and on earth is given to Him. As the Son of God, He has all authority in heaven and as the Son of Man, He has all authority on earth. I like to put it this way:

The Son of God became the Son of Man so that the sons of men might become sons of God!

It means that every believer and any who dare to believe, in faith, can carry the same miracle working power that Jesus had. He has given that authority to man through the believing church. The Bible further tells us that all the fullness of God dwelt within Jesus when he walked this earth and we are complete in Him. If you dare to believe, you too will see miracles in your life.

As Christians we carry His name; we carry His word; we carry His authority and His presence lives in us. These are not just biblical concepts they are a reality.

As I have travelled around the world, all the expenses for travel, the cost of the conferences and seminars, the cost of the crusades, the feeding and transportation of pastors and so on have fallen on me. Not that I have the resources for all this, but the promise of God is that I will always have sufficient for my own needs and for that of the ministry. I do not look to other men to finance this great need. I present my requests to God, and God has used many men and women in providing such need. I do present the needs of others and anyone who is a supporter of our charity, Starfish Christian Trust, will know that I am often asking for the needs of other situations. In addition, I have from time to time, taken temporary work to finance the work to which I have been called and apart from my own personal needs the money has always gone into the work of the Kingdom of God.

On one occasion I took a job driving lorries for a local timber merchant. It was tough work and I was sometimes asked to deliver heavy loads. On most days, there were two loads to take out and I arrived back at the depot around lunch time to collect my second load for the day. There was a man working in the yard who had the foulest mouth – thankfully there was no blasphemy or I would have certainly rebuked him for it. One afternoon I arrived back in the timber yard and he was taking his lunch and so I had to hang around until his break was over and I sat in the cab. Suddenly a voice called out *'Hey! Jesus!'* I looked around to see that he was calling me to collect my next load. I do not recall that I had been talking to him about Jesus up to that point, but the unclean spirit that caused his foul language recognised the truth. *'Christ in us.'*

I took a temporary job with Royal Mail delivering parcels for a few weeks. As I was walking up the hill to my home one Thursday afternoon the Lord said to me, *"I want you to resign from this job tomorrow."* At that time, I had a large telephone bill as I had been trying to support a missionary in France who was having a particularly difficult time. This was before Skype and mobile phones and my telephone bill had rocketed. I presented this need to the Lord and said, *"Lord I need one hundred pounds!"* To my amazement, when I got home there was a letter waiting for me with a cheque for more than this amount. When I went in to work the next day the manager called me in to offer me full-time employment. He could not understand that I had gone to his office to resign. It has been my experience that when God calls He also provides.

I had been to a Fire Conference organised by Christ for All Nations and had received an invitation to join Reinhard Bonke and his team at a crusade in Mombasa. It was a wonderful week and I had a platform area pass and so was able to see close up many of the wonderful miracles that followed the preaching of the Gospel. Tens of thousands of people were at the meetings and the testimonies flowed. It was the New Testament exploding in a predominantly Muslim city. Blind eyes were opened, the deaf were hearing, the lame were walking. Inspiring.

Away from the crusade meetings we were staying in a wonderfully comfortable beach hotel in Bamburi. There was even time for a two-day safari to Tsavo East National Park. It was for me as good as any holiday especially as from there I was to catch the bus to Kitale in the west side of the country – an African journey of some sixteen hours.

I had need of time to reflect on the many miracles that I had seen on this crusade and decided to take a quiet walk along the beach. That was when it happened! Completely unexpectedly! Out of the blue! As I was walking a young man came up to me and without any introduction, simply got into step beside me, and asked the question in these exact words. *"What must I do to be saved?"* This only happens in dreams and daydreams! But here it was on a sandy beach in Mombasa alongside the Indian Ocean. I naturally answered his question and he went on his way rejoicing. When we are walking with the Lord, people can discern Him in us.

There are many areas that were lost in Adam that have been restored in Jesus. For example, God gave Adam dominion over all creation. That includes animals. I do not have a large testimony about this but there was one occasion when my kitchen seemed to be overrun with ants! Armed with the knowledge that dominion has been restored to believers I commanded them to leave in the name of Jesus. It was as if they did a U-turn and walked out and for the rest of the time I lived in that home I did not see another ant in my kitchen. No, I did not use any powders or chemicals! Just His name.

It may be some are still sceptical about how we can command the weather. Bearing in mind that Jesus calmed a storm with just a word we also should be able to deal with the weather when there is a need for the kingdom of God. Life examples can be used to teach and train others. On more than one occasion I have arrived at a church and received

82

complaints that there has been no rain which was overdue and much needed for the crops. I cannot remember where it was now, but in one venue in Africa such an event happened and before each meeting I told the congregation to stand and to pray for rain. I am not sure how much they believed but on the second meeting at the church in brilliant sunshine and clear blue skies I walked to church with an umbrella. When I arrived they started laughing. *"Why are you laughing?"* I asked. *"We prayed for rain. I choose to believe that rain will come!"*

If we do not believe that God will answer our prayers, then we are wasting our time in praying! These people prayed for rain but it was only in hope. Faith is the <u>substance</u> of things hoped for. On this occasion I did not just hope that rain might come but believed that the <u>substance</u> would come and acted accordingly. I believe it was a great lesson for them as the day after I left their area it was reported that the heavens had opened, and they had received the rain that they so desperately needed. It is not a question of praying *"Lord, if it be your will."* We know God's will for all circumstances. How do we know His will? Because He has set it out in His word, the Bible. The Bible tells us that every promise that God has ever made is *'yes and Amen in Jesus'.* In this circumstance there was a need for rain. The particular promise of God to apply in this circumstance is that He will provide all our needs. All we had to do was pray in faith that rain would come. Two little words. 'In faith'.

I believe the prayer quoted above, *"Lord, if it be your will,"* is pretty much a faithless prayer. It is born out of hope and not out of faith. We need to simply find the relevant promise that God has made to fit our circumstances. Once we have found it we simply stand and walk (with no apology for the mixed metaphor!) on the promise that He has made. Coupled with this, I so often hear people say that they are, *"<u>claiming</u> this promise"* or *"<u>claiming</u> that promise!"* We do not need to claim the promises of God. If God has promised then the provision is already made. We simply need to walk in His promises.

Faith is the <u>substance</u> of things hoped for; the <u>certainty</u> of things not yet seen.

One Easter Saturday found me at the Royal Albert Hall in London to listen to a faith filled preacher by the name of Benson Idahosa. He was certainly a man who believed that God would do what He promised in His Word. To me the most interesting thing that he said at the beginning of his preaching was that throughout the meeting some people would see miracles and others would not. This really spoke to me. What he was saying was although we would all witness the same things some people would be sceptical and would not believe what they saw. I am happy to say that I saw miracles that Saturday which greatly increased my faith. I saw blind eyes being opened; I saw a lady get out of her wheelchair; I saw and heard many testimonies to healing. If I had been sceptical it would have been dispelled when I saw the wheelchair lady pushing her chair away from the meeting with great vigour.

There will always be someone to try to disprove that miracles happen today. This is nothing new. There have always been people trying to explain away the miracles, even the established miracles of the Bible. There is a well-known story that God parted the Red Sea so that the fleeing people of Israel might be able to cross in safety. Once they were safely across, the Egyptian army began chasing them through the divided waters. God then allowed the waters to return and the Egyptian army was drowned. A certain sceptic claimed that there is a part of the Red Sea that is very shallow and that the people of Israel must have crossed on a shallow part. His argument does not hold water (pun intended). He was actually declaring a much bigger miracle if the whole of the Egyptian army was drowned in such shallow water!

Many Christians believe that the miracles, healings and other spiritual gifts died with the apostles or once the Canon of Scripture, the finalisation of the books of the Bible, was completed. Somehow, they are missing the point! The Bible clearly says that God is the same yesterday, today and forever. If we do not expect Him to perform miracles and healings how can we also expect Him to bring salvation in answer to prayer? I remember being at a meeting in Birmingham with the aforementioned Reinhard Bonke. Here too I witnessed a lady getting from her wheelchair. She ran around the large stadium with great joy. This was a wonderful healing because she had had so many physical problems. Her healings were documented in a special video and were attested as genuine by her own doctors. Yet still a prominent member of the Church of England Synod spent much time trying to disprove her healing simply because he did not believe that God would heal today in such a way!

We had been ministering on one occasion in western Kenya for several weeks and pastor Protus was travelling with us during this time. It was close to the beginning of the rainy season and he had not yet planted his maize seed. I told him that it would not rain on his five-acre plot of land until we had gone home and he had planted his maize. He looked at me uncertainly but I held firm. Two days later as we were travelling together it started to rain and he was looking rather anxious. We still had another week or so to fulfil our commitments and I reminded him that his land would not receive rain until he was ready. There were African showers of rain every day from then on but each morning the report from Protus as he joined us was that there had been no rain on his land. He later reported that he was able to plant his seed before rain came to his land. Was this according to God's will? Yes of course it was. He is faithful to his promises.

You remember my story of the young evangelist who told me these things do not happen here in the West? Well here is a story that will negate this faithless statement. Let me introduce you to Matthew. He was, and still is, among my close personal friends. One Sunday morning I received a phone call from his wife, Jackie, who was in tears. *"Matthew is seriously ill. He is in a coma. Will you come and pray for him please?"* After church I went straight to the hospital, anointed him with oil, laid hands on him and prayed for his healing. Nothing happened! That was fine. Often when we pray healing is not instantaneous. (Often people do not receive their healing if it is not immediate. They will walk away with the words *"God has not healed me!"* Their expectation is gone along with their faith.) I firmly believe that whilst God does not give us sickness or infirmity, sometimes He delays enabling us to grow in faith.

I love the story of the raising of Lazarus in John's Gospel. The message came to Jesus that Lazarus was sick but Jesus remained where He was for two more days. He declared *"This sickness will not end in death but will bring glory to God!"* When He eventually arrives at Bethany Lazarus is in the tomb having been dead for four days. However, He stands at the mouth of the tomb and commands *"Lazarus! Come out!"* Jesus answered the prayer immediately but the manifestation of the answer was not immediate! It came four days later. This is where faith comes in. Do we respond by saying, *"God didn't answer my prayer"*, or *"God didn't heal me,"* or do we stand in faith confident that we will receive the manifestation of His answer? Faith is the substance of things hoped for. Faith says I will see it when I believe it. Fear says I will believe it when I see it!

Isaiah chapter 53 tells us that when Jesus died on the cross, He not only brought us salvation but that He carried our sicknesses and infirmities, our oppression and the lack of peace. As I was leaving the hospital the Lord spoke very clearly to me. *"Do you believe My word?"* I naturally replied in the affirmative. He proceeded to show me two promises in the Bible. Firstly, that believers will lay hands on the sick and the sick will recover. Secondly that elders will anoint the sick with oil and God will raise them up. He made a promise to me that day that if I stood on His word against all odds that Matthew would recover and God would raise him up. From that moment on, whatever circumstances seemed to surround Matthew, I confessed only that he would recover.

Every day I went to his hospital room and took with me an A4 sheet of paper on which I had printed in a large font a healing promise and taped it to the wall of his hospital room. For three weeks I did this and his wall became plastered with healing promises. This became a tremendous witness to the medical staff. I know others were praying, but in all this time my testimony did not change. Remember, faith is the substance, the certainty, that we will see what we do not yet see.

After some three weeks I had another call from Jackie. Once again she was in tears. *"Stan, the doctors have just spoken to me and they have told me to think about making plans for Matthews funeral!"* As she spoke faith just rose in me again and I said to her, *"Matthew cannot die!"* I was still believing the word that God had given me. Note that I did not say he will not die but that *he cannot die*. Every day Matthew had been lying in a coma and the doctors had not been able to heal him. A few days later was Easter Sunday, the day of resurrection. After church, the Lord told me to take bread and wine, the substances of the communion table, and share it with Matthew. Jackie was there so we shared the bread and wine together and I could only touch it to Matthew's lips. Nothing happened. No change!

I was awoken extremely early the next morning by another phone call from Jackie who was again in tears. This time, however, they were tears of joy. She told me that through the night Matthew had sat up in bed and asked for ice cream. Sometimes we do not always understand how God works, but if we learn to stand on His word we will learn to grow in faith. Why do I class this as miracle? The doctors were talking death. They had no answers. God had promised life. He is the answer.

Sometimes, it seems much easier to pray for others then to pray for ourselves. But the promises of God apply in just the same way to us as it does to others. I learned this most valuable lesson early in my Christian walk. I was walking across our local common, Blackheath, when I was suddenly hit with what seemed an outrageously heavy cold. Suddenly my eyes were watering and my nose was congested. It would have been easy to have resignedly accepted that I was in for yet another head cold. However, I was prompted by the Holy Spirit to rebuke this attack. As I was walking I started making such declarations as, *"I rebuke this cold in the name of Jesus!"* *"My body is the temple of the Holy Spirit and you have no place within me!"* *"The Bible says that we are healed by the stripes of Jesus!"* By the time I reached the bus stop, which was my target, the symptoms had completely lifted from me. Although I may find myself with sore sinuses from time to time, probably because I am a heavy snorer, I have never had a cold or flu since - now more than 35 years.

When I was travelling in Africa with Owen, a young man from my church, he developed the most outrageous head cold. We were obviously travelling very closely together and all the while the devil was telling me, *"Aha! You are certain to catch this cold!"* One day at the pastor's house we were offered tea but there were insufficient mugs. I let Owen drink first and when we were ready for our own drink I deliberately chose his mug. He tried to stop me telling me that I was sure to catch his cold. I told him that I had been hearing this from the devil and I wanted to demonstrate to him that I was not afraid of him or his words or his cold which is why I chose his mug. Needless to say, I did not catch it.

The doctors diagnosed me with prostate cancer some thirteen years ago and was, at a subsequent consultation given three to five years to live. I have never received this diagnosis nor spoken the words 'I have cancer' over me. I remain completely symptom free. They give me regular scans and after two consecutive scans was told that I had a growing shadow on my lung! I took this diagnosis to the Lord before going for further tests. When that day came I was given all sorts of tests but there was no sign of a problem or a shadow. The doctor could only agree with me that it was a miracle. We do not have to accept sickness or infirmity. Jesus carried it on the cross.

I could fill this book with dozens, maybe hundreds of examples of the intervention of God in response to faith. God did not create the earth, wind it up like clockwork and leave us to get on with it! Christianity is not another religion but a relationship with the living God. He so wants to be a part of our lives that He sent His son Jesus to die to make that possible. He wants even more for us. He wants us to live in the same way that Jesus lived and He will fully equip us with the power of the Holy Spirit if we are prepared to believe it to be so. If we fully take hold of this, miracles will happen as we stand in faith.

Chapter 9

A Cup of Cold Water

Gorges is an Iraqi man now living in Australia. Whilst he was in London we became very great friends and spent many hours discussing the Bible. His first language is Aramaic and his insights into the New Testament are profound. Naturally, he often talked about his home in Iraq and the family he left behind when he had become a refugee many years previously. It was probably out of these discussions and our friendship that an opportunity arose to go and see a little of his country for myself. The situation in Iraq was not good. The first Gulf War had not long ended, and the stories reported in the media about the plight of the Kurdish people in the North were severe. I had not formulated a theology about just war, in fact I had not really given much thought to it, but I did have a heart of compassion for the Kurdish people and so I jumped at the opportunity to go.

A mission organisation based in Frankfurt was putting together a road trip and Gorges enabled me to join them. That is how I found myself in my trusty Lada heading for Frankfurt to join a wonderful Iranian man named Wolner. He spoke Farsi and was therefore able to keep us out of much trouble! Without him our communication with the people of both Turkey and North Iraq would have been almost impossible. We loaded a large truck with a tow-bar trailer together with a small bus that had the seats removed. The truck and trailer were loaded with food and clothing et cetera and was packed with bundles of clothing. The interior shell of the bus also had great bundles of clothing which became our bedding on the outward journey. For the most part we kept on driving and sleeping in rotation.

The journey was not without incident. We did not expect trouble in European nations. How wrong we were. We were travelling with papers from the International Red Cross but when we reached the Hungarian border these papers counted for nothing. Whether it was because our final destination was Iraq we will never know. They parked us at the border and they appeared to be simply ignoring us. After several hours, it was time for some action. Wolner and I sat at the wheels of the two vehicles whilst the other members of the team stood in front of them holding Red Cross flags. Wolner and I simply rested our hands on the horns of the two motors to draw attention to our plight. This brought immediate action but not the action we had anticipated. Several armed police came and pulled us from the vehicles and took us to the offices. This action eventually had the desired effect as we explained our plight and we were soon on our way.

We travelled on through Hungary, Bulgaria, the former Yugoslavia and reached the Turkish border. This border presented far more problems. At the Hungarian border the customs officials had sealed the truck and trailer which meant no one could inspect the contents. This was to our advantage as we were also carrying large quantities of Christian literature in addition to the humanitarian aid. The Turkish authorities respected the seals on the vehicles. If they had found the Christian literature they would not have allowed us to take it through their country as this would have been deemed illegal. We were held up at the Turkish border for five days. The authorities were doing everything they could to frustrate us.

It was probably because the authorities were concerned that we might sell the aid items in their own country. They decided we should leave a bond in the sum of US $35,000. It took five days to arrange this and Wolner and I went from the border to Edirne by taxi nearly every day, this being the nearest town and bank. Eventually, the Mission in Frankfurt deposited the sum and we were allowed to cross into Turkey. It was a long journey through Turkey. It took us three days to cross with short stops at Istanbul, Ankara and Diyarbakir before reaching the Iraqi border. What a beautiful country Turkey is. We were not there as sightseers, but our spirit was lifted by the beautiful mountains as we travelled between Istanbul and Ankara. Although there were few incidents on this trip there was an incident in Istanbul when somehow a man got into our bus and stole about $1000. Our last short stop before the border was at Diyarbakir. Diyarbakir is the third largest city in Turkey and is considered by the Kurds to be the capital of Kurdistan. There was a definite tension in the air as we stopped for a couple of cups of Turkish coffee which I am sure was so strong that the caffeine kept us going all the way to the border. It was strange to see that the men in the café were playing a board game similar to our game called Rumikub.

Strangely we did not have too much difficulty crossing into Iraq. We arrived at the Habur Border or as it is also known the Ibrahim Khalil border crossing. Having had so many difficulties coming through to this point it was surprisingly easy to cross into Iraq. The southern side of the border was operated by the PKK, The Kurdistan Workers Party, who welcomed us very warmly into North Iraq.

What a beautiful country. The hills and mountains of North Iraq are simply breath-taking but the destruction that we witnessed all around us almost immediately was most certainly not. The dictator Saddam Hussein, who was the president at the time of the first Gulf War had wreaked destruction on the Kurdish people. It is an old adage that one man's freedom fighter is another man's terrorist and this is certainly true of the Kurds. Their plight has been an almost impossible one. Spread between the borders of Iran, Iraq and Turkey they have no homeland for themselves and in their eyes are fighting for justice and their own natural homeland. (A somewhat naïve over-simplification) Naturally the nations in which they are settled see their actions as terrorism and so there is little peace for them.

What we did find can only be described as the aftermath of a genocide. These people, who were genuine and legitimate citizens in this part of Iraq had been the victims of chemical attacks upon them. Records show that as many as 350,000 men, women and children may have been killed by these weapons of mass destruction. In addition, their homes and villages had been dynamited by aerial attack and there was not much left for them that had not been destroyed. These people were pastoralists

91

but naturally the chemicals had also destroyed their animals and therefore to a large extent their livelihoods.

Thankfully, Wolner was able to speak to them in their language and was able to give us accounts of their situations. Survivors of the genocide were just beginning to return to their homes but they now had nothing. Their homes were destroyed. Their livelihoods were destroyed. The bodies of many of their family members were buried beneath the rubble of their destroyed homes. They had erected temporary shelters some from cardboard, some made with iron sheet and whatever they could find from the rubble. This was not at all sufficient since these were mountain regions and it was still early spring and very cold. We visited three main towns, Mosul, Erbil and Kirkuk.

We were welcomed like long lost brothers. Not just because of the food and clothing that we took but simply because of the knowledge that they were not alone and that at least someone from the West knew of their situation and were prepared to go to them. In normal circumstances I am sure they would have welcomed us into their homes and given us a feast as that would have been their normal hospitality. As it was in some of the homes that we visited they were almost apologetic that they had nothing to offer us. However, several offered a glass of cold water from the mountains. Because of the circumstances I think it would be fair to say it was the sweetest water I have ever tasted!

In the places that we stopped, Wolner by knowing the language, was able to organise an orderly distribution of the aid. People were naturally eager for help but thankfully we were not mobbed, and everyone received at least something from our vehicles. Surprisingly, the situation was different when we came to give out the Christian literature that we had on board. I made a comment at the time that if we had been giving away hundred-dollar bills they would not have fought more than they did for this literature. Wolner was able to understand what a lot of them were saying. Talking of the destruction of their homes and livelihood, what they were saying was something to the effect that if this is what our brother Muslims do to us we do not wish to know about Islam. They

92

seemed desperately hungry to receive the truth. These Kurdish people were so open to the gospel and I know that Wolner made at least one further trip from Frankfurt. Research suggests that there was little effort to reach the Kurds at this time. Maybe it was too far outside the comfort zone of the majority of Western Christians. We did meet one American Christian in Mosul and he was very discouraged. He seemed to have no one to support him and he was just about ready to give up. I do not know what became of him. I sincerely hope that he was able to stay and encourage and reach these dear people.

We did not stay too long. We were there with a purpose and not as tourists. It certainly did not take long for the vehicles to become empty. We were there over the period of Easter. I have a very vivid memory that I am sure will stay with me for ever. We were sitting in a tent which appears to have been supplied or left behind by US forces. There was a stove in the centre and the tent was beautifully warm. It was a clear night with an almost full moon and the moonlight was shining into the tent through the open door. We were sat on one of the bunks and opposite us was one of the Kurdish militia with his AK-47 rifle laid on the bed beside him as Wolner shared the gospel with him. It was a beautiful moment and I remember this man every Good Friday. I do not know who he is nor where he is now, but he is prayed for at least once a year.

Each night we slept at the side of the road in our vehicles. On our final night we slept in what seemed like a layby. We were woken surprisingly early the next morning by a man knocking on our vehicles. His house was one that was still standing and he had made some unleavened bread and he offered it to us for our breakfast. It was a wonderful act of love. I have travelled to many places and seen much hardship and conflict but the one thing that seems a common factor amongst all people is that whatever labels they may have as terrorists, separatists, freedom fighters et cetera, beneath it all, in most situations, they are just fellow human beings wanting to live peaceable lives with their families. Some find themselves in the situation of fighting to achieve that peace and will always respond to acts of love and kindness. I found the same when with the men fighting in the Sudan People's Liberation Army in southern Sudan before it became a separate nation. It is easy as we read newspapers and listen to the television to make severe judgements. Yes, there are those with evil hearts but all of them are those for whom Jesus Christ gave his life.

It was time to start our homeward journey and as we returned to the border we encountered more trouble! Once again it came in the form of one of the Turkish officials. We had, of course, taken video film and pictures of our visit. As Westerners leaving Iraq, their interrogation of us was quite severe and at first we were interviewed by the regular border guards. Wolner had removed his video camera from the case to show them what he was carrying. This was the excuse that we believe they were looking for. Suddenly our whole team was taken to another office which was the domain of a very officious and aggressive guard. It appears that the offence that we had committed was to take video film at the border although, of course, this had not happened. It seemed that underlying our difficulties was the fact that the Turkish people did not want footage of the true situation of the Kurds to be known by the outside world. I believe their aim was to confiscate the video footage and films that we had with us.

We were held there for many hours. Wolner naturally denied the accusations, protesting his innocence that all he was doing was showing the camera to the guard. It seems that he was seen looking through the lens of the camera as if taking film. There was no satisfying Mr Officious. At one time he sat at his typewriter and I assumed he was writing some form of report of the situation or maybe even a confession! When he had finished he pulled the paper from the typewriter and indicated to me that he wanted me to sign it. It was written in Farsi and I had absolutely no idea what it said. I may have been confessing to murder for all I knew. My response was clear, firm and I believe with an odd expletive something to the effect that he must be joking. He was getting more and more angry. People who know me also know that I am not the most patient of people especially in the face of injustice. I was travelling with a team of Americans on one occasion who had a large quantity of electrical equipment for a series of crusade meetings we were to hold in Kampala. I nearly got the whole team arrested as I accused the border guard who was detaining us of corruption! My impatience with Mr Officious at the Turkish border was now beginning to grow. My anger was also growing fast as I stood face-to-face with him and told him that I had had enough of his games. I demanded to see his commanding officer who was responsible for the border station. To my surprise he immediately concurred.

About 10 minutes later the officer appeared. From the amount of braid on his uniform he was obviously high ranking. I explained the situation to him and said how sorry I was to have caused him trouble and that we were in effect not the troublemakers. I pointed to Mr Officious and said that he was the one who had caused the trouble and if he was to arrest anybody then he was the one to be arrested. He listened patiently to our dilemma which had the desired effect. Unfortunately, he told us that the only way that we could be released was if Wolner surrendered the film, which he reluctantly agreed to. It became obvious that this was the only way to break the deadlock. It was now about midnight and we were free to leave.

Even this had its problems. We were released into the area of south-east Turkey, the area where the PKK, the Kurdish separatists were fighting. Following the Gulf War and their treatment at the hands of Saddam Hussein they were highly active and extremely militant in this area and Wolner was more than a little concerned that we should be travelling through this area at night. He knew that they were taking hostages to help their cause. Although there had been reports of the taking of hostages in Istanbul who were subsequently released we were now in the middle of their 'war zone'. He was most insistent that we should not stop for any reason. However, a seemingly good reason came when the young German driving the truck stopped when a dog ran across the road. Within seconds we were accosted by members of the PKK. This could have been an alarmingly difficult and dangerous situation.

Thankfully Wolner spoke their language and was able to explain that we were returning from North Iraq and had been helping their people. This satisfied them and they allowed us to continue our journey untroubled. After all that had happened we were happy to arrive in daylight at Diyarbakir where another large quantity of Turkish coffee was consumed before we set out on the long and comparatively uneventful journey back to Frankfurt. After all we had been through, Diyarbakir did not seem to hold the menace that it had previously.

After Diyarbakir the journey back was without problems. The pressure was no longer on us and we were able to really appreciate the beauty of the countryside. We did stop in Ankara and stayed overnight with a Christian family. It was good to be able to sleep in a real bed even for one night. I cannot remember the name of the family but they had six daughters. I loved the gracious comment that Wolner made that we were entering a rose garden! It was also extremely interesting to talk about the persecution of Christians in Turkey, something that is not often heard about in the West.

In Istanbul, we made another short stop. There were two highlights for me. The first was to eat fresh fish from the Bosporus. The second was a visit to the Grand Bazaar. The most amazing, bustling indoor market area. Although it was a feast for the eyes, with so many spices, dried fruits et cetera for sale it was a wonderful feast for the nose also. I was attracted to a beautiful midnight blue and gold samovar. It took pride of place in my home for about one week but when Gorges saw it, he loved it so much that I was delighted to present it to him.

We retraced our steps back to Frankfurt without incident and I was reunited with my trusty Lada car and after such an emotional journey I was so very pleased to be home. Having given the samovar to Gorges, my only souvenir was the Red Cross flag and an undated letter from them, both of which served me greatly in crossing difficult borders in the future!

Some people think I am a little crazy to have gone to some of the places that I have been. There was around this time an advertisement on television for a certain beer called Heineken. (other similar beers are also available!!) Their slogan was that it reaches the parts that other beers do not reach. I am not advertising for them but a friend once called me 'The Heineken Missionary' because he thought I was reaching those parts that other missionaries did not reach! Quite a testimony! Iraq was not the last 'Heineken moment' as there were many more difficult countries to visit and borders to cross in my future travels. Indeed, it was not long before I was back in Africa again facing yet another war zone!

Chapter 10

Jump in the Pit

Pastor Boaz came from Eldoret in Kenya. I cannot remember when I first met him but he had been working with an NGO in Sudan. He was leading Gospel Flames church in Huruma, a satellite settlement on the outskirts of Eldoret. His knowledge of Sudan and how to get there was invaluable and without him we would never have succeeded in reaching Yei, our destination. At this time Sudan had not been divided and the civil war had been ongoing for more than 20 years. Since my visits Sudan has been divided and the nation of South Sudan has now been born. Sadly, it has not brought a great deal of peace to the region. Pastor Boaz had been working in Sudan as a driver and I believe part of his motivation for inviting me to accompany him to Sudan was that he wished to renew his many acquaintances, but nevertheless it was a fruitful visit. We had to go to the SPLM (the political arm of the SPLA) in Nairobi. A lengthy questionnaire, photos and an interview and we were given a blue pass with which to travel. Without this we would not have been allowed to enter Sudan. It was not an official government Visa but with the south being under their rule and that of their army this permit allowed us to enter. The Sudanese government in Khartoum would not have granted us a Visa to visit the south and the SPLM would most certainly not allow us to enter the south without their permit to enter.

Apart from knowing the dangers of living in the war zone that was Sudan, Pastor Boaz also knew the dangers in his own hometown. I am not sure that Western nations fully understood the implications of insisting that African nations embrace Western-style democracy. I am not fully convinced that it works in the West and it certainly is very fragile in Africa. Party politics has never really worked successfully in Africa as the newly formed political parties divided very much on tribal lines. Each tribe wanted to ensure that the man from their own tribe was successful and instigated their own form of tribal genocide killing thousands and displacing many hundreds of thousands in the process. On one occasion I knew that there were some severe clashes taking place in Eldoret. I was home in London but the media reports were very disturbing. One report highlighted the situation about the killing of many who had taken refuge in a church in Eldoret but an opposing tribe had locked them in and set fire to the building killing more than 30 people inside. I phoned Pastor Boaz and could hear screams and shouts and gunfire outside his home as I spoke to him. The weeks leading up to these elections were extremely dangerous times in Kenya.

The first tribal clashes took place around Christmas in 1991. I had been spending time in Liyavo village, the home of George Opara. The first report of clashes was of a riot in Kitale town where government owned property was being destroyed. On Boxing Day, gunfire was heard at the tarmac less than a mile from Liyavo village and reports came that rebels were coming towards the village to destroy it. The women and children were hidden in the maize fields. I felt completely useless. I could not speak the language and would probably have been more of a hindrance than a help. I decided that rather than be in the way the best course of action for me was to get out of the way - so I went to bed! I slept well and it transpired that there was no such attack. However, George had churches on Mount Elgon where the clashes were particularly fierce. It was a privilege to pay for and send a vehicle into a serious area of fighting to rescue Pastor David and his family. It was probably the most unusual New Year celebration that I have ever undertaken but knew it was no small thing to rescue a family from probable death. Unsure about how these clashes might develop George and I made a contingency plan that I would flee across the border into Uganda and make my way home from there if necessary. Thankfully, I was able to complete the planned programme with a few adjustments but it was an unmistakably tense time.

As is often the case in Africa, travel is not always easy and the trip to Sudan was no exception. A flight from Nairobi to Kampala was no problem and although the flight north to Arua was without problem we did wonder whether there was enough runway for the plane to take off at a mid-journey stop at Gulu! It looked as if the airstrip had simply been put in place in the middle of a maize field. The pilot had the engine revving at full throttle before releasing the brake but we lifted off, skimming the top of the maize as we did so.

Pastor Boaz knew Arua and took us to a fairly secure hotel. This area was the one from which Idi Amin came and like large parts of the north of Uganda at that time was quite insecure because of the work of the LRA. The Lord's Resistance Army was fighting the government of Uganda and kidnapping boys for their army and girls and women for the pleasure of their men! Although it carried the name 'Lord', this army had nothing at all to do with Christianity! Led by two prominent people, Alice Lakwena and Joseph Kony, it is steeped in spiritism. They deceived many and over the years became involved in widespread human rights violations, including murder, abduction, mutilation, child sex slavery, and forcing children to participate in hostilities. It is said that they even persuaded their followers that they did not need arms, but if they threw stones at their opponents these stones would turn into grenades!

It is amazing how easily people can be deceived by spiritual charlatans. In Uasin Gishu district of Kenya there was a man calling himself Jehovah Wanyoni. He managed to gather about four hundred followers who believed he was God. He reportedly had 24 wives, the first of whom was called Mary and he called his firstborn son Jesus! It is not surprising to learn that those who would follow him had to sell all their possessions and give the money to this sect leader. Although it is not funny, I did smile when I heard that he had appointed an assistant God!

Back to North Uganda. We needed to hire a vehicle and driver to take us on the long and difficult journey to Yei in Sudan and Pastor Boaz found a young man who claimed to be a nephew of Idi Amin himself. He was quite a character and thankfully a good driver. He insisted on calling me 'my Mzungu' for the whole of the trip. (Mzungu being the Swahili for white man!).

Ready to hit the road, our driver, whose name I have sadly forgotten, set off for Yei. Surprisingly the Ugandan border checkpoint was several miles from the border itself in a town called Koboko. This was presumably for their security and we had little difficulty passing through. I am not sure that we would call the Sudanese at the border officials. They were presumably a part of the SPLM. It was all very laid-back and because of our driver, who seemed to be very well-known by them, we were soon on the road again. It was a little disconcerting to be told to stay only on the road and not to wander off at any point should we stop as there could be mines and other unexploded ordinance along the way. Looking out as we travelled I saw more than one unexploded bomb that had obviously been dropped by the Sudanese Air Force and had failed to explode.

For the sake of narrative, I will combine my three visits to Yei into one. Pastor Slim came with me on my second trip, and a friend Howard, was my companions on the third. On our arrival, we were met by Bishop Elias. He was a very tall man who had lived in the bush for six years fighting with the SPLA alongside John Garang, who later became the first president of South Sudan. The bishop's wife was, in those days, still a general with the army. As Christians, we sometimes find it difficult to understand the concept of just war. We had many long discussions with the Bishop. He explained how they saw themselves not as an aggressive proactive army with ambitions to make territorial gains. They were fighting to defend their way of life, their families and their faith. For the most part in the West, we have not had to face such issues but if our families and children were being attacked, our wives and daughters being taken for the pleasure of an invading army and our boys were being kidnapped, being falsely converted to Islam and made to fight in the army against us I am sure that we too would not passively sit back and let this happen. He also explained that as the south of Sudan was predominantly Christian they also considered themselves to be defending their way of life against increasing pressure from Khartoum for the whole country to be converted to Islam. He told us that on the frontline they had Christian chaplains who would pray with the troops

101

before battle, not just for success, but that there would be a minimum of bloodshed on both sides.

His first instruction after greeting us was to point out several pits dug around his home and the church and said if there should be an air raid we were to immediately jump into those pits for safety so any shrapnel should pass over us. It made us very aware that we were in a war zone, but thankfully whilst we were there on all three occasions no air attack came.

We were always made to be very welcome and were made to be comfortable at his home. We always had good meetings at the church and in one nearby village the Jesus video was shown. Almost the whole village turned out to watch, especially as this was something of a rarity and following a short talk by Bishop Elias many in that village prayed to receive Jesus as their saviour. On one visit I was asked to hold a unity conference. Over the years, and in many places, I must have held more than a hundred such unity conferences. It was coming from this teaching that my 'Unity' book was written. It appears there were eight different denominational churches in Yei and the leaders from all of these churches attended. It was an encouragement when at a question and answer session at the end of the conference the leader of the Catholic church stood and asked from which denomination I came. I have never revealed at such conferences the denomination of the church that I attend. He was puzzled because at the conference there were Catholic, Pentecostal, Presbyterian, Methodist and other denominations together. He said they all came from different church traditions but that my teaching satisfied them all. It underlines the importance of keeping strictly to the Bible without adding or subtracting denominational doctrine. The pure Word of God will satisfy every man.

On my third trip, when I was accompanied by Howard, a part of the itinerary was to cross into the Congo. We made the same difficult trip from Nairobi to Arua, again accompanied by pastor Boaz. The Democratic Republic of Congo has a large Eastern border and this was a completely different part to that of Goma that I had previously visited.

Here the Civil War was still raging and with hindsight it was probably a fairly dangerous venture. I always check the British and Foreign Commonwealth Office travel advisories and this whole area and in particular this border crossing was an absolute 'red' do not go warning. I had explained some of the difficulties to Howard before we left London but felt it best not to give him too much detail about this aspect of our travel as I did not want him to be too nervous during the visit.

He has recounted several times since we have been home how he was amazed when Bishop Elias came to me before the journey started and reported serious repair needs for the four-wheel-drive vehicle before we could cross over into the Congo. His amazement was that I almost casually handed over $600 to put the vehicle in order. It was not part of our budget, but I have always believed that in all circumstances we meet the immediate need and do not worry about later needs. To put the words of Jesus into my own words, he said we were not to worry about tomorrow as tomorrow will take care of itself.

We were late leaving because of the repairs, and further held up because there was a bushfire that had straddled each side of the road. We eventually managed to get through this without difficulty and by the time we arrived at the border it was in total darkness. There was no electricity in such a remote area, the only light coming from a warming fire. Howard and I sat at the fire whilst Bishop Elias held long conversations with people that we could barely see in the dark. We could see their vague shadows in the firelight but were not party to their conversation. It transpired that the Bishop knew these SPLA soldiers on the border personally through the time he had spent in the bush. He and his SPLA friends were negotiating with the rebels in the Congo for our safe conduct to Aba, our destination. Their conversations were long and I am sure that they were old friends and were recounting their many experiences in the bush. Eventually in the darkness of midnight we were on the road again. I had not shared with Howard what I knew to be happening until we were safely back in Nairobi. I did not wish to trouble him too much. He did confess to me later that he was somewhat nervous to be sat in the back of the truck flanked by two incredibly young boy soldiers armed with AK-47 rifles. We arrived in Aba in safety in the middle of the night.

In spite of our late arrival, we were given a typically African warm welcome and even at that time of night tea was produced which added much to the welcome. In spite of the insecurity, life here seemed to go on relatively undisturbed. I am sure they had experienced moments of danger and confusion but during the time we were with them there were no incidents. Sometimes people make the comment that they think I am brave or courageous to go into some of these places but in all honesty when you are confident of the promises of the Lord and His calling there is generally no great fear. We held several more meetings and once again the Jesus video was shown with great effect. There was a very solid response to the call of the gospel at the end of the film. It was not long before we started our journey back to Yei and on to Arua. We said our goodbyes to 'My Mzungu' and had a smooth journey back to Nairobi.

Chapter 11

The Power in His Word

For many years people have been encouraging me to write a book about my 'experiences' as I have travelled to many nations and been involved in extraordinary situations. I had until now resisted as I did not want to write just another autobiography that chronologically reads "and then… and then… and then…" But neither do I wish to write a theological book although my hope is that by writing about my experiences I can encourage others to learn and grow in their own faith. These chapters do give many examples of my travels and I hope that as I have travelled on in my faith venture you will find encouragement as you continue reading.

If I were to ask any Christian *'would you like to produce more fruit in your life?'* I am sure they would reply positively. My understanding is that the production of spiritual fruit is not about struggle and stress in an effort to develop more faith. It comes out of a simple love-walk and relationship with the Lord Jesus and a simple trust that what he says he can do he will do. He uses the example of a vine. In John 15 he says that He is the vine and we are the branches. *"If you abide in Me and I in you, you will produce much fruit."* The secret to a fruitful life is in the abiding. Christianity is not just about going to church on Sunday. That can never fully satisfy. If that is the sum of your Christian life you are missing the point. It is about a living relationship with Him seven days a week.

The power to heal the sick or to perform miracles does not come from ourselves but from the one who dwells in us as believers. His power in us and our faith in Him can enable us to do the impossible or indeed as I have entitled this book these things are 'HIMpossible'. It is a great partnership.

One of my favourite traditional readings at Christmas comes from John chapter 1. It starts *"In the beginning was the Word, and the Word was with God, and the Word was God."* Jesus, the Word of God living in us, speaks through us. When we speak according to His word with the *dunamis* (this is the Greek word meaning power or authority from which we also get to the word dynamite) of His life and combine it with faith the HIMpossible will happen. Let me give you a couple more demonstrations of how the power of his Word can be effective in us.

I was sitting under a banana tree drinking tea, one of my favourite occupations in Africa! A message came from a nearby village that both a man and his wife were ill. The husband was crippled and the wife had fallen seriously ill. Just where we were we prayed for this couple to be healed and carried on enjoying our tea. A couple of days later we were driving past their home returning from a meeting in Kolongolo and we heard them shouting. We stopped and saw that they were jumping up and down with joy. Not only was the wife free from her illness but her crippled husband had been healed. The power that brought healing was a combination of the word of God coupled with the faith of those who prayed. It reminded us of the story of the Roman Centurion who came to Jesus asking for prayer for his servant who was sick. When Jesus said he would go to his home the centurion simply said I recognise the authority by which you speak. Just say the word and my servant will be well.

Sometimes, healing may come through the faith of those who hear. There was a time when Peter and John healed a crippled man because they saw that **he** had faith to be healed. The faith rested with the one who had the need rather than the one who was praying on this occasion. On one trip, I had finished my itinerary and my thoughts were now simply on boarding the bus back to Nairobi for the flight home the next day. I was told we had been invited to another home in the village that evening and to be honest I did not want to go. I had finished my work and was simply ready for home. Of course I had to go and when we arrived they asked me to bring a word of God to the family. Frankly, I did not want to do it and suggested we wait until after we had eaten in the hope that they would forget this request. Of course, after dinner they asked for the word and with little grace I brought out a simple story about the woman who was healed when she touched the hem of Jesus's garment. I followed this by telling them it was their decision as to how close they wanted to be to Jesus. There was no grace in my word, neither did I have any particular faith or expectation. But in spite of all this, three ladies knelt saying they wished to be prayed for to receive Jesus! The power was still in the Word of God but the faith was in those that heard it. It was not in myself as the one who delivered it! It was also a great lesson in humility!

A combination of God's word and man's faith will be efficacious! Just as the Bible shows Jesus to have the name of 'The Word of God' and we consider the Bible to be similarly 'The Word of God', how can we separate the two. To my understanding they are the same thing in different incarnations - in a different form.

Jesus said of himself *"I am the Alpha and the Omega; the beginning and the end; the first and the last."* If we combine this statement with his name as The Word we can see and believe that Jesus has the first word and Jesus has the last word. All other words come somewhere in between.

If I have a serious legal dispute I may go to a lawyer who may give me legal representation and speak into my situation. I will make full use of the services of the lawyer. However, I do not rely solely on his advice but rest my case with the word of God. Isaiah 54:17 states

> *"No weapon formed against you shall prosper, and every tongue which rises against you in judgment you shall condemn. This is the heritage of the servants of the LORD, and their righteousness is from Me, says the LORD."*

If we are walking in the light and we know that we are speaking the truth about our situation then we can choose to leave our vindication with the Lord. Jesus is the 'Alpha word' and the 'Omega word'. The word of a lawyer or the diagnosis of a doctor may be true, but it comes somewhere between the Alpha word and the Omega word. If we let Jesus have the last word, and stand firmly on that word, then faith can operate and we will see miraculous results. Let me give you a personal testimony.

I wrote earlier that I have been an outpatient at the Guys Hospital in London for over thirteen years with a diagnosis of prostate cancer. That I have prostate cancer is their word. That is their diagnosis. I do not argue with their diagnosis but I do not take it as the final word. I let Jesus have the final word. His word says, to put it simply, I am healed. (1 Peter 2:24 - *By the stripes of Jesus, you have been healed'*) Do I still take the medication that they give me? Yes! Do I trust that the medication is doing me good? Yes! My answer to people is that I keep taking the medicine but trust the Lord. In thirteen years I have never spoken the words, "*I have cancer!*" That would be to own it. My testimony has always been one of healing and not one of disease. I will never speak sickness, illness or infirmity over my own body and I will never speak it over another person. Is the cancer still in my body? The doctors say it is. Do I argue with the doctors or tell them they are wrong? No! I simply walk in trust in the word of God. Whether the cancer is in my body or whether it is not I live and walk completely free of symptoms. If I receive a negative diagnosis, I do not necessarily say that the diagnosis is wrong, but I break the power, I break the curse of that diagnosis. As I wrote earlier, at one early stage the consultant told me I had perhaps three to five years to live. Now some nine years since that diagnosis I am still completely free from symptoms. I am not dead but wonderfully alive! I walk by faith in the Omega word – the last Word - and not by sight.

I had a dear friend who has now gone to be with the Lord. It was through him that I first started my missionary travels. On his return from a ministry trip to Africa he picked up a virus which developed into a post-viral syndrome and a diagnosis of M E. This terrible disease just got worse and worse until eventually he became bed ridden. It was so sad to see him slowly wasting away. Nothing that the doctors could do would bring him any relief. Many people prayed for him and over him including a well-known international healing evangelist but all to no avail. I will not say this was the only reason that he was not healed, but he completely owned his infirmity. He would continually talk about '*my infirmity*'. I tried on several occasions to counsel him that the infirmity was not his but he continued to own it and continued to deteriorate until he went to be with the Lord. I believe he would still be alive today if he had changed his confession? Only God knows. But I do believe it was a certain barrier to him receiving his healing. Only God has all the answers!

There must be more than twenty occasions when I have been asked to pray specifically for a family that is unable to conceive. Particularly in Africa, it is always assumed that it is the fault of the wife. When I am praying if it is possible I like to pray for the husband and the wife together. I remember on one visit in Kenya George stopped at a house and asked if we could go and pray for the young wife. Of course, I forgot all about this until on a later visit I was dedicating about 10 babies. As I was praying for each child suddenly George stopped in front of one and said to me, "*This one is yours!*" I looked at him uncertainly but he reminded me of the occasion we had prayed for the young wife and she had conceived. Later I joked with George, "*If that baby was mine, then I must be the father of many black babies!*"

In my travels I have taken hundreds of open-air crusade meetings. It is my delight. I love to be able to share the word of God with whoever might listen. At the end of every meeting after I have called people to receive salvation through Jesus Christ I will always follow this by praying for the sick. I have seen hundreds, probably thousands, of people healed by the power of the word of God. Why do I also pray for healing? At the end of the gospel of Mark we read that certain signs will follow those who believe. And then the final verse of the gospel says that the disciples went out and preached everywhere, '*the Lord working with them and confirming the word through the accompanying signs*'. Here is a clear confirmation of the link between the preaching of the word of God and healing and miracles. As the disciples preached the word, and one must believe that they combined it with faith, then the Lord confirmed his word. As we read through the Acts of the Apostles we see that they moved with great power and signs and wonders. This is the testimony of the early saints and it could, in fact should, be our testimony also.

One of the most famous chapters is Isaiah 53. From it many people see and understand salvation. But the verse promises so much more. The complete restoration of all that was lost in the Garden of Eden by Adam is restored in Jesus Christ (the second Adam).

> *Surely He has borne our* **griefs** *and carried our* **sorrows**. *But He was wounded for our* **transgressions**, *He was bruised for our* **iniquities**; *The chastisement for our* **peace** *was upon Him, And by His stripes we are* **healed**.

That is why after preaching the word, I will offer to pray for the sick and infirm. In this way I have seen some wonderful healings. One of the first miracles we saw in Kenya was a man getting out of his wheelchair and walking. In Uganda, there was a girl, about eight years old, who had some sort of wasting disease which caused her whole body to stink. She was completely healed and stood on the crusade platform singing 'Yes, Jesus loves me' - that one really brought tears to my eyes. In the Philippines an old man who could barely breathe started running to a far-off tree and back and returned with no heavy breathing.

Many of the 'big named' evangelists like to go to the big cities where they can gather a huge crowd. I have found that because of this there is often more success in the small towns and villages were no visiting evangelist has been. On one visit, I was travelling with pastor Slim and we held a crusade meeting in an extremely small out of the way village called Eshisiru. It was amazing to see a crowd of well over a thousand people crammed into the marketplace for what was an immensely powerful meeting. At the end of the meeting a young girl named Mary was brought to me who was born deaf and dumb. She had never spoken and had never heard since birth. After prayer her hearing returned and as we whispered in her ear, her speech returned. The first word she ever heard and the first word that she ever spoke as we whispered in her ear was the name "Jesus". Her friend, also named Mary, sent me a letter about six months later and confirmed that her friend Mary was learning to hear and to speak. It is always good when we get confirmation of what the Lord has done.

It is, of course, not always at the crusade meetings that we pray for the sick. I was teaching a Unity Conference in India and the subject did not include any teaching about healing. However, a deaf young man was brought to me at the end of one session who, like Mary, had been born deaf. Once I had prayed for his healing his father said he can hear but not very loudly. On this occasion I felt the Holy Spirit saying to me that if he got all his hearing back immediately the sound would be too much for him to bear but that he would receive his full hearing step-by-step.

In a healing meeting in Pakistan (we cannot use the word crusade as historically this has negative implications) a paraplegic man was brought to me for prayer. If I am honest I sometimes waver when there is something major like this. However, I did not hesitate to pray for him and whether it was my faith, his faith or simply the mercy of the Lord we heard that the next day he had been healed and was in fact climbing trees.

One of my favourite stories concerns a boy with mental troubles in India. He was not at any of the crusade meetings that we held in a cluster of villages. The pastors provided transport to bring people from many villages around to hear the preaching of the gospel. The Indian people are very reserved and do not often publicly acknowledge healing et cetera at the meetings. The local pastors hand out prayer slips and testimonies are reported back. One such testimony was from a couple and they wrote that they had been to about to about twelve hundred meetings at their various Hindu temples but had never heard the gospel. They gave their lives to Jesus that night and when we prayed for the sick, they prayed for their son to be healed. They took the healing word as truth and 'expected' their son to be healed. When they arrived home their son was fully healed and in his right mind. As a result of this story, and because everyone in the village knew the boy, many in that village gave their lives to the Lord and a new church was begun.

I could recount stories of countless others healed by the combination of the word of God and faith. We walk by faith in the Word of God and not by sight

There is always a faith element to be exercised if we are to experience the Word of God being seen in our lives and in the lives of those around us. We do not have to work up great faith to see God at work but simply believe. This was often the message of Jesus. *"If you believe, you will see the glory of God." "Do not be afraid, only believe."* I have already written that the power by which we minister rests in His Word. This is a promise for any believer and not just those in ministry. When Jesus said we must become like little children, he was not saying we must become childish. A little child is like an open book. If a parent, or perhaps a teacher, tells them something they will simply believe. I have witnessed a young boy of just two years old who could have no theology of healing or even a great understanding but had heard that Jesus can heal. I saw this young boy lay his hand on an older lady. I do not know what he prayed but I am sure his prayer was uniquely simple, and the lady was instantly healed.

I have written that I have prayed for many thousands of people to receive their healing, and especially in open air meetings and ministry times in churches. Many times people are instantly healed and many times the healing is not seen instantly. In the latter cases I have so often

111

seen people return to their seats or homes somewhat dejectedly because they have not been healed. Sadly, many of them go back with a confession, *"I have not been healed! Jesus didn't heal me!"* This is something that I try to address when the ministry time is over. The words *'I have not been healed'* are words of faith! Unfortunately, they are not words of faith in the Word of God but in their current situation. (This is walking by sight and not by faith in the Word of God) I try to encourage them to put their trust in God's Word and change their confession to *'I have been prayed for. I will recover! I will recover! I will recover!'* This has resulted in many hundreds of people being healed, even if the manifestation of their healing was not immediate.

One reason that so many prayers seem to go unanswered is that people choose which parts of the Bible they wish to believe. There are some difficult passages and some teaching that does not square with modern 21st-century living. These are problematic in terms of seeing the fulfilment of the promises of God in our lives. The Bible clearly says that *'all scripture is God breathed (inspired by God).'* That means that even those passages which we do not understand or are out of sync with our modern-day living are to be believed and trusted. In talking about areas of sexuality, for example, many will say, *'Well, Paul was a man of his time. Today we have a much better understanding of these things.'* Effectively, this is saying that we know better than God! If we undermine the value of just one verse of the Bible, we destroy the integrity of the whole book. When God inspired the writing of the Bible, he knew it would be challenging not only to our own post-modern way of thinking, but to many beliefs and cultures over the millennia. The way to see your own faith grow is to accept the integrity of the whole book whatever your personal views. Jesus said, *"Heaven and earth will pass away, but my Word will never pass away."*

(This does not mean, for example, that we reject, isolate or condemn people with different sexuality, beliefs, culture et cetera. Jesus gave his life for all. If we reject and condemn others, we are not doing the work of the gospel, but the very work of Satan himself!)

Some years ago I heard a story of a dear lady who lived to a very old age. When her relatives were sorting out her possessions, they came across her Bible. It was very worn and had obviously been well used and well loved. As they looked through it, they could see written in the margins in so many places simply the words '*T and T*'. It was some time before they realised what she had written. She was a faithful follower of Jesus and in his Word. The words simply meant '*tried and tested!*' Unless we try and test the promises of God, we will not see their outworking in our lives.

The Bible talks of faith as a spiritual gift. Every believer is encouraged to have trust and faith in God's Word, but there are occasions when he will give a supernatural certainty that what we are praying for will be received. God is the same yesterday, today and for ever and there is no shadow of turning with him. The God of the Bible has not changed; neither has His word. He will work in any situation and in any place.

Many of my anecdotes are from my travels around the world, but he is also working here in the West. As I have been preparing this book, I received a wonderful testimony of healing in a situation where God gave me a specific 'gift of faith'. I now belong to a wonderful Pentecostal church in Bexleyheath, Kent. The level of faith of the members is high and there is a great environment of faith in which to minister. A few weeks ago, a young man was brought to the church in a wheelchair, unable to walk or to lift his arms. At the end of the Sunday morning meeting several of us were asked to pray for this young man. Initially many prayers for healing were offered, but then God gave me a 'gift of faith' that this young man would be healed.

I have heard many preachers tell the story of how Peter walked on the water towards Jesus in a violent storm. As soon as Peter took his eyes from Jesus he started to sink and cried out for Jesus to save him. I knew that the Holy Spirit was telling me to command this young man to look at me. He was obedient to this command. I helped him, with others, to stand but continued to tell him to look at me. Not that there was any merit in my appearance, but he needed to be focused and not look at any other circumstance around him. He started to take faltering steps as I continued to command that he looked at me. Later that morning he was able to walk unaided to the car which had brought him to church. I was not present when he returned one Sunday morning. But this strong and upright young man came to the meeting. The pastor greeted him as someone he had not met before but was soon told that this was the same young man. He was now strong, upright and preparing to start playing football again. Hallelujah!

One of the things that I have learnt over many years of trusting the Lord and trusting His Word is that we need to practice and learn to let go of our problems and requests. I liken our prayer requests to someone holding them in his hand and lifting them to the Lord and saying something to the effect that *'Lord I give this need or problem to you!'* When they bring their hand back down it is as if they are still holding on to the problem or need that they have just 'given' to the Lord. *"What should I do about this problem? How will I get what I need? I cannot see any way through this difficulty!"* The reality is that we say that we have given the problem to the Lord but continue to worry as to how we will get through. If we believe that God is able, that He is the God of the 'HIMpossible', we need to learn to stop worrying about the 'hows' and 'whys'. We need to learn to get out of God's way so that He can answer our prayers or supply our needs His way. We have given the problem to Him so let Him do the worrying and let us wait for the solution. In this way too, we are walking by faith as we wait for the Lord Himself to answer our prayer.

There is no circumstance in our lives that we cannot change if we line up our testimony with the Word of God. I have written in an earlier chapter that Jesus came to destroy all the work of the devil. What was lost in Adam is fully restored in Christ. There is a faith venture waiting for you! Know God's word and simply believe.

Chapter 12

Back to Africa

My love affair with Africa continued grow. I am a firm believer that God's promises, unless otherwise indicated, are unconditional. From my earlier employments I knew that I had a small pension provision but decided it would be far better spent in the kingdom of God. I cashed in that pension and returned to Africa. The Bible's promise for provision does not stop at the age of 65! He still continues to provide wonderfully. Although it would seem that my travelling days are predominantly over, I am living in a beautiful brand-new purpose-built flat. I have an amazing view of a tree covered hill. And although it is not a Lada, I still am driving an exceptionally reliable car!

I was so grateful to John and Jackie, missionaries living in Nairobi, who gave me a home for the seven months that I based myself in Africa with my pension money. They had a beautiful home in a secure compound in Ngumo. It had a small outbuilding which they called the servant's quarters. I changed the name very quickly to the 'garden flat' and sometimes referred to it as the prophets' room. They had a growing adopted family and I loved being Uncle Stan. They are now living back in England and the family are fully grown but I am still Uncle Stan! I was a little surprised recently when staying with a family in America that I had evolved to Grandpa Stan! I guess it was inevitable and bound to happen as years went by.

I was able to renew acquaintances with many of my old friends and I worked hard, probably too hard, to try to meet their every request. I went with them to many churches around Kenya and beyond. In addition, I met three special people and greatly enjoyed adding their homes, churches and countries to my itinerary. The first was Pastor Jeremiah. I met him at the Nairobi Pentecostal Bible College where I often took morning prayers. He was a Congolese refugee and had started three Congolese refugee churches in Nairobi. I was a regular speaker at his churches and we grew to become great friends. We are still the greatest of friends, and through Starfish Christian Trust we have been able to help his ministry grow now that he is back in Uvira. It was clear from the start that he loved the Lord but you could discern a great sadness within him as he loved his people and at that time longed to go back to his home in Uvira.

He had a large family and for the safety of his own family he could not return to D R Congo. One day he asked if we could travel together to visit his people in the refugee camps in Tanzania. There were two refugee camps, one at Lugufu and the other at Nyaragusu. Both camps were close to the border of D R Congo and the journey was amongst the toughest I have undertaken in all my travels. We took a Missionary Aviation Fellowship (MAF) plane to Mwanza, Tanzania on the south side of Lake Victoria and from there a train to Tabora. We then had to wait 24-hours for the night train west. We stayed several nights in Kigoma even holding several church meetings but our mission was the two camps. The next morning we started out on one of the worst roads that I have ever encountered. I have sometimes joked with my African friends that it is whilst travelling on the rutted and pot-holed roads that they learn to dance! It was neither a short journey nor a comfortable one but to compare it with the plight of the refugees we had nothing to complain about.

It took several hours to arrive and I was quite surprised by what I saw. It was obvious that these people had been in the camp for many years. It was almost like a small town in appearance except there were none of the usual things you would find in a town. There were no shops or businesses. They had precious little money and possessions. They were dependant on NGOs for their daily provisions. The only building that I could see that was not built as a temporary home was the church. It seems that the church was certainly very organised and had a large congregation amongst these people. Our objective on this occasion was not specifically evangelism. We felt it was mainly to enable Pastor Jeremiah to be able to visit some of his family, his many friends and the church that it seems he had helped to construct in the past. It was truly clear how much they loved and respected dear pastor Jeremiah. They fell about him with hugs and kisses as one would only do for a long-missed friend.

Our second purpose was really to simply encourage the refugee people and let them know that they were not forgotten by the outside world. I am not sure how much the outside world truly knew about their plight, but at least they were happy to receive visitors from the West. I have been in many situations that have been so humbling over the years. For example, on several occasions as a visitor people have wanted to wash my feet. This to me is one of the most difficult and humbling experiences but to refuse could be a sign of disrespect. These poor people, who were totally dependent on the aid organisations which were feeding and caring for them, insisted on killing a goat and feeding us. This was a great honour for us and a great sacrifice for them. Some reading this may feel that we should have refused the goat but it would have been a great offence and I am sure that for them it was a great feast. Occasionally in other situations when I have preached in a rural church someone will press a shilling into my hand. It will not buy me anything but it is probably a great sacrifice and would bring a great blessing to the giver. To refuse would cause great offence.

We did hold two meetings, one in each of the churches. The Congolese have a strong reputation for singing and I have heard many of their choirs in my time. There was one song, the words of which I did not understand but it was sung with such feeling that it moved me to tears. It started with the words 'Baba Mungu…' Their emotion touched me so much. I asked what the song was saying and as best as I remember it was, *Father God, why have you forgotten us? Why have you left us here? What have we done to offend you?* Even as I write, the memory has brought tears back to my eyes. So moving. I made two visits to the refugee camps and had little to give them. The NGOs were feeding them and looking after their physical needs but it was a privilege to be able to at least take some spiritual encouragement – and Pastor Jeremiah!

Many years later pastor Jeremiah was able to return to Uvira and what he saw was a devastated land and a somewhat demoralised people. His family had moved to Kampala which was closer to home but he felt it was not yet safe for them to return to the D R Congo. I have had the privilege of going twice to Uvira and have seen how hard he has been working to restore the faith of the churches. In a very short time he had built a new church in Uvira itself together with a small orphanage. He has also purchased a large plot on the side of the hill overlooking Lake Tanganyika to build a Bible school where he is able to train men to become pastors and build new churches. I held several meetings in his churches. One of the most memorable was an open-air meeting at Sebele another long and bouncy road away. Several hundred people were gathered for the day and what a wonderful day it was. Many people responded to the call of the gospel and as always many also responded for prayer to be healed. At that time the people of Sebele had no church building and we met under a large avocado tree. Recently, through Starfish Christian Trust (more about this later), we were able to send funds to enable them to cover their new church building with iron sheet.

The best way to travel to Uvira is through Bujumbura in Burundi. It has not always been the safest of journeys and our Foreign and Commonwealth Office advice has almost permanently been not to travel this way. The border crossing is tense and very insecure. I am not sure what it is about some of these difficult borders but they always seem to have a fair assortment of shady -looking characters! But the Lord is always travelling with us and it is through faith in his protection that I have been able to travel to many places of insecurity.

Burundi itself has suffered many years of civil war. When I first met Pastor Jeremiah at the Nairobi Pentecostal Bible School I also met Pastor David who lived in Bujumbura. He was the second of the three good men that I met at that time He arranged for me to hold meetings in this small capital city. Most of his churches were in or around Bujumbura itself and in addition to powerful meetings in many of his churches I was also able to hold a pastors' seminar. As usual, I provided transport, accommodation and food for these pastors for three days with about a hundred and twenty participating.

Pastor David knew that I was going to be visiting the United States shortly after my return home. With this knowledge he said something which surprised me very much! He said, *"Brother Stan, when you go to America will you please tell them to stop feeding us!"* I was puzzled by his request until he explained further. He told me that when people from the West, and particularly from America, visit his churches they have large sums of money and they hold seminars similar to the one we held. They bring in many pastors, leaders et cetera and just as I did, they feed them and accommodate them. The problem that Pastor David was trying to express was that he lived permanently in Bujumbura. When he wanted to bring his pastors and others together for teaching he was unable to do so because he could not afford to feed them et cetera. The expectation amongst the church leaders has become such that a seminar is not just about teaching but an opportunity to have a few free meals. For the most part his 'complaint' was quite valid. I did write a small article and submitted it to a couple of Christian publications in America, but I am not sure if it was ever published.

On this visit we went up into the beautiful mountains. From Bujumbura we could hear constant gunfire in the mountains and on more than one occasion a grenade was exploded in the city. Miraculously, for the days we were in the mountains we heard no gunfire until we returned to the capital. This was my experience on two occasions. As Psalm 23 tells us, *'Even though we may walk through the valley of the shadow of death, we shall fear no evil!'* It was another wonderful example of faith in action as we went into rebel territory. We stayed at a place called Bukirasazi and held a wonderful crusade meeting for three days. They had built a large platform in the open space with a large banner across the front. I could not read what it said but three words stood out very clearly... **Dr Stan Gain!** What could I do? Everything was prepared; leaflets and posters were everywhere all declaring me to be Dr Stan Gain! I could hardly negate all their efforts and so for three days I became a doctor! I do have an honorary degree in theology from a Bible school in Australia but the nearest claim I can make to even a university degree is BA. And this, in my translation, stands for 'Born Again'! Thousands of people attended over the three days and many new churches were established. One such church was planted by pastor Joseph who lives in Gitega and through this visit we too have become very firm friends.

Burundi is listed as one of the five poorest countries in the world. Pastor Joseph and his family really struggle in their work for the kingdom of God. I have since visited him in Gitega on three occasions and seen his work and also his struggles. On my first return to Gitega I was shocked to see just how much havoc the Civil War had wreaked. In the town centre most of the buildings had been razed to the ground. It had been a violent and bloody war. It had forced me to flee from Bujumbura on one occasion. I was staying in a hotel in town. The electricity had already been cut but this was not a rare thing in this part of Africa. In the middle of the night I was awoken by the sound of a mortar shell exploding close to the window of my hotel room. The rebels had hit town during the night and fighting was fierce. I moved to a room which did not have an outside window and spent the rest of the night in darkness listening to the sound of gunfire. There were two Americans also staying in this hotel and in the morning we put our nose outside the front door. All we could see was much fighting still continuing in the street and bullets being fired in all directions. At a great price and at great speed we were able to persuade a taxi to 'run the gauntlet' to the airport. It is really no exaggeration to say that we were dodging the bullets! I was able to find a flight back to Nairobi and to safety.

I have mentioned it a few times, so let me add this point introduce you to Starfish Christian Trust. It was established in 2012 and one reason was to consolidate and give a degree of accountability for the work that I was doing. In addition, some other ministries were taken under its wing. Through it we have been able to continue to give solid financial support to many of these ministries. It is supported only through donations and the goodwill of others but has been able to keep supporting the work that the trustees have seen established. It is a fully registered charity in the UK. Every penny that is given to the trust goes to supporting these works. Administration costs et cetera are met out of charitable support given by the British government in the form of Gift Aid.

We are often asked why we chose the name 'Starfish.' It comes from a simple story.

> *"A man was walking along a deserted beach. A storm had washed up thousands of starfish onto the beach. As he walked, he could see a young boy in the distance picking something up and throwing it into the water. Time and again he kept hurling things into the ocean. As the man approached, he could see he was picking up one of the starfish that had been washed up on the beach and, one at a time he was throwing them back into the water.*
>
> *The man asked the boy what he was doing. The boy replied," I am throwing these starfish back into the ocean or they will die." "But", said the man, "You can't possibly save them all, there are thousands on this beach. You can't possibly make a difference." The boy smiled, bent down, and picked up another starfish and as he threw it back into the sea, he replied "I made a difference to that one!"* (Original Story by: Loren Eisley)

From this we have developed what we call the Starfish Principle. We cannot change the whole world, but we can make a difference one life at a time.

I met pastor Joseph on one of our visits to Bukirasazi. He lives in Gitega, and we soon became very firm friends. With him I travelled to the border of Tanzania where a large community of returning refugees were being settled. For a time, they were receiving support from NGOs but for unknown reasons that support was no longer being given. Pastor Joseph explained that the United Nations were satisfied that they were settled and simply withdrew. They had their good statistic and were not concerned beyond that. He explained that the soil was of extremely poor quality which compounded the poverty of the refugees. Pastor Joseph had established a church among the refugees, and we helped him to put in place a self-help scheme. A small loan would enable an individual to start a small business, maybe planting maize or brickmaking; perhaps to buy a sewing machine or to start some other small industry. As the recipients of the loans make a small profit they slowly return a little to enable another person to establish a small business. It is small help, but it does help these people to become less dependent.

It was a joy to return with him to Bukirasazi. There he had been building, brick by brick, a new church building. It was a pleasure for the Trust to be able to supply iron sheet to put the roof over their building. It is always a fear that they will build so far and when the rains come if they cannot protect the walls the inclement weather will destroy their work. It is so important that they roof their churches as quickly as possible. In addition to visiting his growing churches it was always a pleasure to hold open-air crusades. In Bukirasazi we held more large meetings (this time, my doctorate had been taken away from me!) and my understanding is that the churches in that area have grown again as a result.

There is an amazing group of drummers called the Royal Burundian Drummers. These have become known far beyond the borders of their small country and they have travelled far and wide internationally. A search on YouTube and you will surely find one of their performances. They put on a very lively show of traditional Burundian drumming. They came with us from Gitega to a roadside town, Maramvya, and drew an exceptionally large crowd as was usual with their performances. They were performing to gather a crowd and as a result of preaching the gospel to the large open-air gathering another church has been formed. I understand that this church is growing well.

During my final visit to Burundi, I was taken to a plot of land on a high hill overlooking Bujumbura. Pastor Joseph had purchased this plot and his plan was to build a 'headquarters church' for the whole ministry. His

122

plans were ambitious by Burundian standards. The trustees felt that the building would be too ostentatious in such a poor area. The scale of dimensions of the building were scaled down. We were so thrilled when a local church, St Mildred's, Lee, partnered with us in building what was still to be a mighty fine Sion Chapel. It looks over the city with pride and I am sure has made a great vantage point for praying over the city. As a result, a solid relationship is forming between Starfish Christian Trust and St Mildred's who recently financed the building of a boys' dormitory and ablutions for an orphanage in India.

That whole region of DR Congo, Burundi and Rwanda has seen some bitter fighting and I am sure every reader is aware of the terrible genocide that took place in Rwanda in 1994. I cannot remember how I first met Pastor Theophile. It may have been through my website that we first made contact. I visited Kigali on three occasions. He was my host on two of these and it was through him that I learnt much about the tragedy of the genocide. A brief and simplistic history.... The Tutsis are the minority tribe but held probably 90% of the power and important positions et cetera. The Hutu eventually rose up against the Tutsis and reports say up to one million people, mainly Tutsis, were slaughtered. The issues were much more complex but this is not the place for a history lesson!. Pastor Theophile recounted to me how he had lost all but eight members of his family - and African families are not usually small.

Whilst I had several church meetings, I do not want to focus on them. It is difficult to imagine how one would cope with losing such a large number of family and friends. It was clear that he carried a great sadness but in conversation with him it was clear that he had found it in his heart and through the power of Christ to be able to forgive those who had slaughtered his family. The power of forgiveness is a mighty power. Unforgiveness does not bring pain to the offender, but if we hold on to bitterness, anger, resentment, and unforgiveness it can have destructive and negative effects in our own hearts. It is so important for us to forgive however we may have been hurt if we wish to live in freedom. How frequently do we pray the words of The Lord's Prayer? *"Forgive us our trespasses as we forgive those who trespass against us"* There are so many who hold unforgiveness in their hearts for a past hurt and yet ask the Lord to forgive them in the same way (i.e. unforgiveness) that they carry.

I can remember a meeting in a village on the shores of Lake Chioga in Uganda where I preached on unforgiveness. Even as I preached, the Holy Spirit was bringing conviction into the hearts of the congregation. He was showing them areas where they needed to release forgiveness. It was clear that many of them were in spiritual bondage. There was much healing and deliverance at that meeting. This is not an unusual result when forgiveness is preached.

Pastor Theophile took me to the Holocaust Museum in Kigali. It was a most moving time. Underground there are several extremely large metal containers and within them are the bodies of countless thousands of those who were slaughtered. He was not able to know in which of the containers his brother was laid to rest, but he stood silent for several minutes in remembrance. The museum gave an excellent account of the events of the genocide. It was brutally honest and especially in the way that it recounted how the United Nations, and particularly the French, had been sterile in defending the weak.

This Holocaust museum did not just tell the story of their own genocide but the history of genocide throughout the 20th Century. It certainly covered the Jewish Holocaust of the Second World War even to the extent to show how the British had abandoned its mandate to establish the Jewish state of Israel that had been promised through the Balfour Declaration. Seeing this was a step towards my returning to Israel to visit Yad Vashem, the Holocaust Museum in Jerusalem. I write a little more about this in Chapter 14

Chapter 13

Odds and Pieces

One difficulty of writing auto-biographically is that it can so easily become just a series of 'what happened next'. I have tried to avoid this and therefore to keep some variety in the way my story is presented. As I am writing many anecdotes come to mind which do not quite fit the context or the flow of my writing. I have included many stories of miracles and healings; many stories of lives being changed and many stories of adventures. It has been great joy even remembering so many people and places. I have included some but left out many more but thought a chapter of odd stories would be amusing and in some cases bring glory to God.

People often ask me if I have eaten strange foods. Over the years I can say my only answer to this is 'Yes'. On one occasion we were invited to the home of the local MP, Dr Noah Wekesa. He was a rich man with some 2000 acres of land and perhaps 2000 head of cattle. It was a real joy to be seated at a 'rich mans' table after day upon day of eating chicken, rice and sukuma wiki (a kind of kale so called after the Swahili for week - wiki - because it is eaten every day of the week!) We sat at a table full of delightful foods and included were several jugs of soured milk. This was a bit like drinking plain yoghurt and it was quite tasty. As I was nearly through my second glass I made a mistake and asked a question. There were little black pieces in the milk and I asked Dr Noah what they were. After his reply I drank no more! He told me that it was charcoal and its purpose was to help to kill the worms! Aaaargh! It may seem a strange habit but I soon began to take worming tablets available from the local vet before leaving Africa for home.

I have mentioned before the people of Pokot. A lovely pastoral people whose wealth is counted mainly in goats. They have a delicacy which in their own language is called 'yesterday'. This is milk which they store in large gourds. They spit in it to encourage fermentation and then store it inside their mud buildings for up to 30 days. This being their delicacy it is often given to guests. As a guest in so many Pokot homes I have had to drink many a cup of this unpalatable milk. It is full cream and when poured comes out more in lumps than as liquid. It is various shades of white and cream with a hint of green and as you drink the lumps somehow flow down your throat. Many a time when with Pastor Simon, we would end up in a Pokot house and sit on stools in the kitchen and I knew what was coming. Invariably I was correct as I was handed yet another mug of this so-called delicacy. I decided on one occasion that the best way to drink it was to glug it down in one go as fast as I could. Big mistake! As soon as my back was turned they refilled my mug. Another Aaaargh! On one occasion a young pharmacist was travelling with me and said she really could not drink it and would I help her. It is sometimes hard to be a gentleman!

Once, having taken a meeting at a church in the depths of a wood in Moldova, we sat down to a meal set outside in such beautiful surroundings. On the table in large jugs was a substance that looked like coconut milk. It was certainly not this. It was the sap from the beech trees. Apparently, each mature tree could produce as much as forty litres of sap without damage to the tree. It was not an unpleasant taste and I washed our meal down with two large glasses. What I did not know was that it was one of the most powerful laxatives that I have ever known. The pastor and I spent the rest of the day rotating in the use of the facilities! A great pity I had no resources for marketing this most efficacious product!

Maybe one more food story to complete this section. I was visiting my old friend George Opara in Liyavo and I suspect we were, as usual, sitting under the banana tree drinking tea. Not far away I could hear a sort of drumming and what sounded very much like children singing. I asked George what this was and he smiled and told me, "*Kumbe kumbe! Termites*". I went to see and the children were sitting happily on a termite mound banging sticks and pouring water over the mound. There were termites flying everywhere. It seems that the termites get confused and

126

think that it is raining and out they come. Whilst they are sometimes collected and cooked in a kettle it was with great joy that the children were eating the creatures alive. Needless to say I was offered some of these termites and thought that if the children could eat them with such relish then maybe I could eat at least a few with them. What do they taste like? I think the only word I can think of is earthy. I smiled as I remembered a song from my childhood about an old lady who swallowed a spider – that wiggled and jiggled and tickled inside her!

Sometimes things are not always what they appear. I have mentioned my time at Lake Chioga in Uganda and I was asked to hold an open-air meeting in the village square. It was a good meeting but I guess as an evangelist I was a little disappointed that only one person responded to the call of the gospel. However, everyone around me was exuberant in their joy at this one man. The Bible says that there is more joy in heaven over one sinner that repents. The joy must have been close to the same joy as that of the angels. It was only on enquiring about this situation that they told me that this one man was the local witchdoctor. His salvation would have a profound effect on the spiritual life of the whole village. In contrast, a few days later I was in Kigali, Rwanda and holding many meetings. After one meeting the local witchdoctor was not happy with the message and while I was sitting in the car ready to leave spat profusely into my face. Yuck!

As with the witchdoctor in Chioga I have heard of several stories where the Lord will take hold of a man who is quite central in a community. One such man was George Washington! I am not kidding you that was his name. He was obviously the 'clown' of the village. He wore a T-shirt with the inscription, 'Sex Instructor - First Lesson Free'. As we were to baptise several people that day I could not help but smile that not only had I baptised George Washington but George Washington wearing such a T-shirt!

I wrote earlier that I have never been a fan of the 'prosperity doctrine'. I do not deny that God wants us to prosper, but I believe that in biblical terms the word prosperity is not seen through worldly riches alone. For many years I have lived without income. I have travelled to and through more than seventy nations. In that time the Lord has provided not just for my own needs in travelling and hotels et cetera but also to finance the crusade meetings and seminars. This has included feeding, accommodation and sometimes transport for those who attend. I have never had much in my bank, and when I have it does not stay long as there is always a need to be met by one or another. I will say that in all that time I have never gone without. I have never sat down to an empty table, I have always been nicely clothed, always had a comfortable home and always had enough for ministry needs. I believe I am prospering.

There is a song in the musical 'Fiddler on the Roof' where Tevye asks God *"Would it spoil some vast eternal plan, if I were a wealthy man?"* In a similar manner I once told God how useful it would be if he were to give me a million pounds. Not for my own use of course but for the work of the kingdom (although maybe I would have started flying business class!). His reply was that he had given me much more than a million. It was just that he had not given it to me all at once. It is probably true to say that over the years the amount of money that has passed through my hands for my own needs and for ministry is probably closer to two million pounds. I believe I am prospering. Prosperity in the Kingdom of God is not reckoned in what I have but on what my heavenly Father has. His 'bank account' will never run short. When Jesus needed money for the temple tax in Jerusalem he sent Peter to fish and a coin was found in the fish's mouth to pay the tax. On another occasion he said that the Son of Man had nowhere to lay his head. No one can doubt that Jesus had all that he needed for his life and for his ministry. He prospered.

One day pastor Njiia met me in town and was overjoyed that he had a speaker coming to his church from Nigeria to talk about money and giving. To him, this was an opportunity for raising a good sum for the church or possibly for himself. The meeting came and the Nigerian preacher surely spoke about money. By all accounts he spoke enthusiastically about the 'so-called' prosperity doctrine. At the end of the meeting, as it was told to me, the preacher opened his briefcase and encouraged the people to put into practice what he had been teaching and to give generously. This they did. He thanked them and prayed with great gusto. He then closed his briefcase and went home with all the money. I understand pastor Njiia was not a happy man that evening.

In Africa it is unusual for a man to be single. Many times when people hear that I have never married they look somewhat surprised. I was drinking tea in the hotel in Kitale town one evening and a pastor came to visit. He was somewhat concerned about my marital situation. He had the best of intentions when he asked me if I had seen a certain lady in his church who had no husband. He told me she was a wonderful Christian lady and also a fine cook who would look after me well. If I were to pay a dowry of thirteen cows I could take her as my wife. I politely declined and not just because I have never owned even one cow.

One day I was scheduled to go to a town called Chepchoina to hold three days of meetings with the pastors and also to hold a crusade. I will not say that I heard the voice of God, but I had an extraordinarily strong sense in my heart that I should not go. I told pastor Simon that I could give him no practical reason but that I would not be going to Chepchoina. He was somewhat surprised and a little disappointed but accepted my words. As my next meetings were to be in Nairobi, I took the Akamba bus back. The next day I bought a copy of the Daily Nation newspaper and saw that there had been serious trouble in Chepchoina and some thirty people had been seriously injured or killed. Jesus told us that His sheep know His voice. It is for me rare that I hear an audible voice, but I have learned to know when He is speaking to my heart. I have many good friends and when they phone me I know their voice without them announcing their name because I have spent many hours with them. I know their voice. In the same way it is only as we spend time with Jesus through his Word and in prayer that we learn to know His voice.

I believe I have often encountered angels in my time. I have mentioned already my experiences on my journey in Soviet Union. Often when walking in the streets of London late at night I have seen what looks like possible dodgy situations from gangs of young people. I always ask for angels to protect me and even if I cannot see them I know by faith that they will protect me. After one trip in Africa I had been travelling with Jan. He and I have become great friends and he is now a trustee of Starfish Christian Trust. This was before the days of digital cameras and so my 35mm film was taken to the chemist. On receiving back the film, I was looking through and to my surprise in one photo there was a 'white man' who we had never met. He was walking behind me as I was preaching. I said nothing to Jan as I was showing him the photos and as soon as he came to this particular picture he said in a surprised voice, *"Who is that?"* He was pointing to the white man in the photo. We discussed it and both concluded that we had not encountered any white man on this trip and certainly not in the meeting in which he appeared. We came to no other conclusion than that this was an angel.

On another occasion, a young man who I will not name suddenly became strongly addicted to heroin. He had had no previous experience with illegal drugs. It later transpired that when he was a child he had been given diamorphine as part of his hospital treatment. We could only conclude that this laid a foundation for an addiction which was lying latent. The devil will use any means and any weakness to entrap us and we were all surprised by his sudden addiction. One evening, we were at a wedding reception at the church and he suddenly said he had to leave because he had an urgent appointment. We knew that he was going to a rendezvous to buy more drugs. We prayed for him there and then that the Lord would send angels to frustrate him and prevent him from meeting his source. He later recounted that he was held up by a motor accident on the road in front of him. Because of this he found a telephone box to phone his contact but said there was a man inside talking. Suddenly the man was no longer there and when he went to call his supplier he was too late and missed the appointment. We believed then, and I believe now, that God answered and sent angels. The Bible tells us that all angels are ministering spirits sent to aid those who will receive salvation. Soon after, this young man was delivered from his addictions and is, to my understanding, still faithfully serving the Lord.

There is a very tiny ant in East Africa called siafu. Although it is so small it has the most painful of bites. They march in columns and I have seen them in action on two occasions. It seems that they will 'march' into the roof of a building and then drop down into the room. Anyone who is beneath receives dozens, if not hundreds, of their tiny painful bites. One night we were staying on the slopes of Mount Elgon when my hosts started to light a wall of fire. Apparently, an army of siafu were marching towards our homestead. They had built the fires to deter them and turn them away. Needless to say my imagination was too active and I slept very little that night.

One thing that amuses, and often frustrates me, is that I have found that the people of East Africa will answer a question with the answer that they think you want rather than with the correct information. For example, if you ask them how far we have to walk they will say, *"Do you see that tree? It is just there."* When you arrive at the tree they will say, *"You see that house? It is just there."* I am sure I walked almost 10 kilometres to one meeting which was 'just there!' I smiled on another occasion when I was given the reply, *"It is not far but it is a distance!"*

Have you ever been caught in an ill-disciplined scrummage in a foreign airport waiting to board the plane? I was returning home from a trip to India with Rich and sitting in Hyderabad Airport looking at the building numbers of people waiting for the flight to be called. It would be another absolute melee. I looked across and saw that they were beginning to gather the 'infirm' for pre-boarding. In a moment of inspiration I suggested Rich went across to the staff member responsible and tell him that I had hurt my leg and had trouble walking. My scheme worked. I was called over and I put on my best limp. I was sat in a wheelchair and wheeled onto the plane by Rich ahead of the melee! Am I getting older? Certainly! Wiser? Probably!

My purpose in this chapter is to just present series of mini pictures of life lived by faith. We were holding a crusade meeting in the West of Kenya and all the time I was preaching a lady was shouting abuse at me. At the end of the meeting I was a little disturbed that the hosts were beginning to collect money from the people attending. Firstly, I believe that the gospel is free and secondly I had already agreed to pay for all the expenses of the crusade. When the money had been collected I called this abusive lady onto the platform and I gave her all the money that had been collected. My hosts did not seem too happy with this but the lady was delighted and also at the final time of praise and worship was there singing and dancing with all her might. I understand that she subsequently gave her life to the Lord.

In a similar vein, I was preaching in Uganda and a young lady came to the front before the platform and started stripping. I chose to ignore her and continued preaching and a couple of pastors led her away. I was later told that she was receiving ministry from the local pastors and that in previous encounters this lady had walked completely naked. Never a dull moment!

One of my favourite healing testimonies comes from Tanzania. I had been about 10 days in Mwanza, and in the lunch hours was holding a series of meetings in a local cinema. The meeting had long finished and we were preparing to leave when a little hunched lady came in and made her way slowly to where we were standing. She had wanted to be at the meeting but was not able to travel fast enough to get there. It transpired that she was riddled with cancer and had come for prayer. I was happy to pray for her and laid hands upon her to pray for her healing. As is often the case I was not aware that she had been instantly healed until that evening I was talking with the pastor. He told me that she was indeed completely free of cancer. There had also been a supernatural happening for which I have no explanation, but once I had finished praying for her my hands were covered with a thin film of the most fragrant oil. I have not smelt anything so beautiful since and I was naturally, reluctant to wash my hands for a while. I do not know why the Lord sometimes gives us these manifestations but know they serve a purpose that only He knows. Maybe it is to simply encourage.

Now to complete this chapter, as I am often asked about some of my encounters with wildlife I thought a few anecdotes would be enjoyable. Spiders are prolific and sometimes I have seen some fairly large and evil looking eight legged beasts. One such was when I was standing preaching in fairly long grass in Rwanda. I looked down and coming towards me was a very thick, hairy spider. I later learned it was an extremely dangerous one indeed. I must confess that it interrupted my preaching while the spider was dealt with in an appropriate fashion.

Not every wildlife encounter was negative. I was travelling with young Owen in Nairobi National Park where our attention was drawn to a giraffe that at first looked to be in trouble. As we watched we realised it was giving birth as the poor youngster fell from a great height to the ground. It was fascinating to watch as the mother, shielding it from the sun, was doing all she could to get this young one on its feet before one of the big cats came along. It was amusing to see these long legs flying around all over the place until he was able to stand and walk.

I have been fortunate to have made several visits to the game parks and seen all of what are called the big five game and of course many of the other wonderful animals. My most endearing memory is being stranded in our vehicle by a herd of some three hundred elephants. Thankfully, they did not see us as a threat as they ambled past us. From massive bull elephants to little baby elephants trotting alongside. It took about forty minutes for this whole herd to pass us. Fascinating. In the animal orphanage attached to the Nairobi Game Park we were approached on one occasion by one of the wardens. He attached himself to us and I am sure was looking for a nice tip. He did get a handsome tip as he enabled us to go into the enclosure with two beautiful cheetahs that had been raised by hand from kittens. To be able to pet them as one would a domestic cat was truly amazing. We could feel the roughness of their tongues as they licked our hands – a little disconcerting given that this roughness is to enable it to lick all the flesh from the bones of their victims.

One last encounter that I will relate was an opportunity of a lifetime. I was with pastor Theophile in Kigali when he announced that we had a free day and would I like to go and see the silverback gorillas in the rainforest of Volcanoes National Park. It was expensive but it took me no time at all to accept this invitation. These beautiful animals are a protected species and continually tracked. The rainforest lived up to its name and by the time we reached the gorillas I was soaked to the skin. A minor inconvenience to be able to spend an hour in the presence of such majestic animals. As we approached the area we were suddenly accosted by a huge male, Quite startling. Our guide knew him and the gorilla knew our guide and after they had exchanged a few 'gorilla' noises we were able to spend some time with them. To be just a few feet from the massive male sitting eating bamboo shoots and eyeing me quizzically was brilliant. To have a little baby virtually running over my feet! What do I say? The only sad thing was that my hotel room had been broken into and my camera stolen. Ah well!

I guess I have just chosen a handful of different individual stories and anecdotes and experiences. When I have so many stories to tell it is difficult to know which ones to include and which ones to leave out. As people asked me to write about my experiences, I thought it will be good to write about some of these in anecdotal form.

Chapter 14

I am not Political!

Ever since I had the vision of the Second Coming of Jesus whilst standing at Megiddo in Israel I was becoming more and more unsettled about the way our nation was being absorbed into the European Union. I was beginning to understand that as we were approaching what the Bible calls The Last Days, there appeared to be compelling reasons to believe that the prophesied Antichrist would come out of a revised Roman Empire. It was clear that this revised Roman Empire would not follow the exact same boundaries as the first Roman Empire of biblical times. This is why I prefer to use the term 'revised'. It was clear that as more and more regulations were coming out of Brussels and Strasbourg and as our respective Prime Ministers were signing more and more treaties we were moving closer to a federal Europe. This was a far cry from the Common Market that we had been conned into accepting in the referendum of earlier years. I use the word conned, because when ex-Prime Minister Edward Heath was asked if he had a federal Europe in mind when offering the nation entry into the Common Market he replied simply, *"Oh yes! Of Course"*. I also believe that it is God who establishes nations and their boundaries and we were giving up our nationhood and sovereignty. We had lost our empire very quickly but it seemed we were being subsumed into an unknown undemocratic organisation.

One of my early questions was how and why our 'Empire' had so quickly evaporated. I was asleep in my delightful mud and wattle house in Kenya when I was awoken by the Lord. He told me that if I wanted an answer to this question I was to go to Yad Vashem, the Holocaust Museum, in Jerusalem. It was not long after I got back home to London that I quickly booked a flight to Tel Aviv and a few days later found myself at the Yad Vashem Memorial. I had visited before and it is a very fitting memorial to the 6 million Jews who had been exterminated by the Nazi regime. The children's memorial is particularly moving. This unique memorial, hollowed out from an underground cavern, is a tribute to the approximately 1.5 million Jewish children who were murdered during the Holocaust. Memorial candles, a customary Jewish tradition to remember the dead, are reflected infinitely in a dark and sombre space, creating the impression of millions of stars shining in the firmament. The names of murdered children, their ages and countries of origin are continually recited in the background.

As you walk through the main memorial there is a pictorial history before you reach the exit. It tells the history of the Holocaust through the war and beyond. It documents the way in which the British blockaded the return of the Jews to the land. These poor Jewish survivors from out of the Holocaust had for the most part made their way over the mountains to the Mediterranean coast with the hope of reaching the land that has now become Israel. They were, I am sure, spurred on by the promise made by Lord Balfour, then Foreign Secretary, that a home for the Jewish People in Palestine be established. It is recorded in NBC News that *"After Germany, many of the passengers in the ships heading for Palestine were eventually detained in military camps in Cyprus along with other Jews deported from Palestine."* Many of this hopeful group of refugees were eventually taken back to Germany where they were also held in camps. Over half of 142 voyages were stopped by British patrols, and most intercepted immigrants were sent to concentration camps.

As a nation we had it in our hands to establish the nation of Israel, but we washed our hands of the whole situation and handed this responsibility over to the League of Nations, now the United Nations. I believe our failure to keep the promise of Lord Balfour and our failure to establish Israel was the beginning of the end of our empire. One year after backing away from our responsibility towards the Jewish people, India gained her independence and over the next 20 years most of the nations that had formed part of our empire also became independent. As we were declining as a nation so we were losing God's blessing.

In the old Testament, when a nation rebelled against the way of God it was taken into captivity. I believe that in those days we as a nation were slowly being taken into a form of 'captivity'. We had broken faith with the Jewish people and were becoming more and more integrated into the European Union. If we remained we would in time lose our identity and individuality as a nation and have as much say in the world as, say, Rhode Island or Arkansas do as small states in the USA.

As I began to seek the face of the Lord to see if there was any way our nation could begin to regain its sovereignty which it had so foolishly abandoned I felt he gave me a strategy which to some seemed crazy. That did not concern me. I would sooner be considered crazy by my fellow men and be obedient to the Lord. What was the strategy? It was what I eventually called "*Joshua Walks*". In the book of Joshua, when the people of Israel were faced with the heavily fortified city of Jericho God gave Joshua a strategy for the downfall of this huge city. Joshua was commanded to walk around the city for seven days with all the people of Israel. On the seventh day he was to walk around seven times and at the blowing of the shofar the walls of Jericho fell, and the city was defeated.

Naturally it would be impossible for me to walk seven times around the European Union, but I could walk around the political heart of each nation and the power centres of the Union in Brussels and Strasbourg. The more I prayed, the more I developed an adaptation of the strategy that the Lord gave to Joshua. I was to go to every parliament of the European Union and walk around each seven times. In addition, I was also to walk around the Parliament buildings of the European Union in both Brussels and Strasbourg.

I copied the same plan for each nation. For each circuit of the fourteen non-UK national parliaments I had a different spiritual exercise. These were as follows

137

1. The first time around I spent simply in praise. Sometimes aloud and sometimes silently depending on the circumstances. But praise I certainly did.

2. The Lord gave me Psalm 2 as the Scripture for the intercession. On the second circuit around each Parliament I would recite this Psalm over and over for as long as it took to complete a circuit. I read the whole Psalm aloud.

    Why do the nations rage, and the people plot a vain thing?
    The kings of the earth set themselves, and the rulers take counsel together,
    against the Lord and against his Anointed, saying,
    "Let us break Their bonds in pieces and cast away Their cords from us"
    He who sits in the heavens shall laugh; the Lord shall hold them in derision…

3. Going around the third time I was praying to break the influence of the Bilderbergers and others who were very unhealthily plotting to suck all nations into their vile form of globalisation. In the case of the UK it was through the European Union.

4. Many agreements and treaties were signed by our Members of Parliament and Civil Servants without reference to, and without mandate from, the people. My prayer was to break the power of these agreements and treaties on the fourth round.

5. The Bible tells us to pray in the Holy Spirit. It tells us that the Holy Spirit helps us when we do not know how to pray, and this was my intercession on the fifth circuit.

6. When Joshua circled Jericho it was undoubtedly spiritual warfare. I saw these circuits in the same way and therefore my sixth encirclement was praying to

release warrior angels to battle in 'Heavenly Places' around the buildings and bring success to the intercession of the first five circuits.

7.   What other the way could there be to complete each Joshua Walk than the way I started with praise and thanksgiving?

On 1st January 2001 with a shofar on my shoulder I set out for my own Parliament buildings. It was too much to walk seven times around my own Parliament as it would have involved going over Lambeth Bridge back around and over Westminster Bridge seven times. I walked around once and when facing the buildings from across the river I blew the shofar. It drew some rather interesting looks but obedience to the Lord is always preferable. I did not take the shofar to other Parliaments as Joshua only blew his on the final circuit of the seventh day.

In addition to the 15 parliaments I also walked around the European Parliament buildings in Brussels and Strasbourg. It made sense to me to finish the intercession on 31st December 2001. I was again at our own Houses of Parliament with one more circuit and one final blast of the shofar from across the river and over our seat of government. After I had blown the shofar I clearly heard the Lord speak to my heart and say the intercession was complete. In 2001 there seemed absolutely no indication that our nation would ever leave the European Union. The only talk in the media was about further loss of sovereignty and further integration into what was rapidly becoming a federal state. My testimony and my faith were clear and unwavering. That we would one day leave the EU and become an independent, sovereign nation once again.

People laugh, or if they are polite smile when I say I am not a political figure! In the same year I felt I should also do something even more practical and support the one movement that seemed to be opposed to our membership. I found myself as a parliamentary candidate in the elections of May 2001 with the newly formed United Kingdom Independence Party (UKIP). It was really quite bizarre. There was barely any organisation for a very embryonic political party. I found their website and there was a button to hit that simply said *'Stand!'* I hit the button and did not expect such an immediate response. Within 30 minutes, I received a phone call from a rather excited lady. She asked me if I was able to put up the £500 deposit needed for a Parliamentary Candidate to which I responded positively. That was it! No interview. No selection committee. No police check. I was the parliamentary candidate for UKIP for the Greenwich and Woolwich Constituency!

Never was there a rawer candidate. I had no idea what to do. I did at least find some guidance on another page of the website. I was my own agent! I was my own leaflet delivery team! I was very much a one-man band. I was taken aback when I was accosted by a Christian friend who berated me for standing for a racist party. This was a slur often thrown at people who wanted to leave the EU. This was not the case. All we wanted was control of our national security and borders. I have always said that we should be a compassionate society and welcome genuine refugees.

It turned out to be extremely hard work. Thankfully, I was sent enough leaflets to cover each home in the constituency and I was able to get these delivered through the Post Office. As my own agent, I needed to find 10 people to sponsor me so that I could become the official candidate. The hustings were good fun. I was able to enjoy them as I knew I had the same chance of being elected as the proverbial snowball in hell! As a minor candidate most of the questions were fielded by the candidates from the major parties. This was probably a particularly good thing as I had absolutely no idea what the policies of "my party" were. It was a fascinating experience to see the election process from the inside and to be at the count. Unsurprisingly, I lost my deposit but did pick up several hundred votes!

Following this election, I came under pressure to start the South East London branch of UKIP. I was somewhat reluctant but about 20 people turned up to our first meeting. It became one of the most militant and active branches in the country. We invited the infamous(!) Nigel Farage to address one of our meetings and our membership was growing. One of the UKIP candidates for the Mayor of London came from this branch. Probably better to say no more about this as he later changed his name and his gender! I stood again in local council elections and for a second time for parliamentary elections in 2005 with similar results! I decided this was enough and thought I would no longer find myself politically involved. Especially at the loss of another £500 deposit!

The Lord was not finished with me on the political front! The Christian Peoples Alliance is another small political party. Under the leadership at that time of Alan Craig it was having some measure of success having gained three seats on the council of the London Borough of Newham. There were no other opposition parties to the Labour Party and therefore the CPA became the official opposition. When the election came for 2010 I was urged to submit my application to become their parliamentary candidate for the constituency of West Ham. The Council and Parliamentary Elections were scheduled to be held on the same day and Alan was to stand for the seat of Mayor. He felt if there was a parliamentary candidate covering the council seats it might increase his chances.

It was a comparative luxury to be part of an organised team with a constituency office. Sadly, in the election held right across the country the small parties in the local councils suffered very badly. The numbers going to vote almost doubled compared to the numbers that voted in local council elections. The CPA lost its three members on the Council, Alan was not elected Mayor and I lost my deposit for the third time! I subsequently became a member of the National Executive and for two years took on the role of treasurer. I am not sure how much influence I had on their policy, but the CPA did change from become Europhile to Eurosceptic. Not bad for someone who claims to be non-political!

The 23rd June 2016 is a date that I will never forget. The Americans have their 4th July but 23rd June will for me be our own Independence Day. It is the day when the British people were given the opportunity to decide whether they wished to remain in the European Union or leave. Most of the media, and especially our own biased BBC were strongly predicting that as a nation we would vote to stay in. For some 15 years I had been telling people that one day we would leave the European Union. It is a foolish man who ignores the Lord when he speaks to his heart. The Lord had spoken to my heart back in 2001 that one day we would be leaving and my testimony every day was unwavering. As happens with all major elections coverage of the results are televised throughout the night and broadcast as they are announced. My expectation continued to be that this was the day that we would vote to leave the European Union. I am not sure how many people expected this to be the result, but I was standing firm on the word that the Lord had given me "Intercession complete!"

The next night starting at around 1:30am the results started coming in from around the country. I was glued to my TV and in contact with many people by telephone and SMS texts. The early results were beginning to indicate that the vote was going to be to remain in the European Union, but I continued to tell people *"No, we are leaving!"* At 30 minutes past each hour there was a news bulletin which gave an update of the news and comment of people from each party and of course from the European Union. From around 4:00am the result was beginning to swing in the opposite direction. And following the 4:30am newscast the following announcement was made on BBC television *"The BBC announces that the decision taken in 1975 by this country to join the Common Market has been reversed by this referendum to leave the European Union"* I was elated. My phone hardly stopped ringing and that day I received many text messages and emails mostly in the form of congratulations, but one or two who were not happy with the result were far from gracious.

As I write the final details are not yet agreed but the final day of our leaving is now set as 31st December 2020. Exactly 20 years to the day since I first blew the shofar over the Houses of Parliament on the first day of 2001. I have not particularly concerned myself with the terms of our leaving. *I am not political!* My intercession was simply about us leaving. Although the details were not a part of the intercession, I will say I am disappointed in the way our politicians have handled the issue. However, for me it was a great lesson in faith. For 15 to 20 years I stood on the word of God that the intercession was complete; that we would leave the EU. Circumstances often would indicate that this would not happen, but faith is the substance of things hoped for. For me in these circumstances the substance was the vote to leave.

Chapter 15

Wider Still

I must be honest in saying that I am not the greatest fan of many aspects of modern technology. Oh, without doubt it is very practical and has its uses but it has a great many disadvantages and can be very time wasting to the point of addiction. I do embrace it where I find it useful. I am using technology to write this book for example. Instead of my usual two-finger typing I am dictating to my computer and my words appear on the screen. It does sometimes give me a smile when I try dictating foreign names and places. E-mail has certainly made life much simpler. When I first started travelling, a letter to Africa would take many days to be delivered and I could wait sometimes three or four weeks before the reply came. Now I can be in an Internet café in Kitale, Kenya arranging and even paying for my next trip to America. Great advantages.

Like many people, I started with a simple Amstrad connected to a dot matrix computer. Although a fairly basic machine I did master it and on one occasion was able to write an individual letter to every Member of Parliament, six hundred and fifty two-page letters and envelopes, detailing how in their legislation they had effectively broken every one of the 10 Commandments and concluding that as a consequence we cannot expect our nation to prosper. (I told you I was not political!) I had a varied and interesting post bag for the few weeks following. I tried to keep up with computer technology inasmuch as it would help in my work, upgrading to the point where I could develop my own website with the help of a friend Mervyn. When something went wrong technically I was like a dog with a bone trying to sort it out and on more than one occasion I was surprised to hear the dawn chorus as I had been up all night challenged by a problem. Over the years many people were led to my presence on the Internet by the Holy Spirit and I started receiving invitations from all over the world to visit and minister. For the most part I would graciously decline but occasionally I felt prompted to respond. Sometimes the response led to a single visit and on others to lasting friendships which remain today.

One such visit was to the Philippines at the invitation of Pastor Ludyvino. He lived in a small village called Maigo on the northern coast of Mindanao Island. He was on the board of the Anchor Bay Evangelistic Association, a network of more than 300 churches around the Philippines and particularly on the island of Mindanao. They were holding their annual conference and I was invited as their conference speaker. I loved the Philippines from the moment I first stepped off the plane at Cagayan de Oro. It is a beautiful country with coconut palm trees exploding in praise almost everywhere you look. Maigo was to be the base for my three-week visit. My window overlooked the South China Sea and our travels to several churches along that coast was a real joy especially as my diet consisted largely of seafood and fruit. The seafood is abundant, and I ate some fruits that I had never seen before and whose names I still do not know. One I do remember – durian – which when you cut into it has a most revolting smell but the fruit is really sweet. Pastor Ludy's sister made a most delicious mango milkshake for me every morning that we were at home!

The journey to the conference was interesting. I was warned it would take all day to travel. After we had been on the road for about five hours, I was instructed to wind up the windows and keep fairly low in my seat. We had entered the area that was highly infiltrated by the M I L F, the Muslim separatist group that was fighting to make Mindanao an independent Muslim country. I understand they have now changed their name and associate themselves with ISIS. They are highly dangerous and are known to take Western hostages. It seemed that the Anchor Bay had their headquarters and Bible School in Cotabato, one of their strongholds. On my return to Manila my taxi driver to the airport asked me if I had had a good stay. I told him I had been on Mindanao and he was incredulous. When I told him I had been to Cotabato he very nearly crashed the taxi. It seems that nobody goes to that area except the Heineken missionary!

The theme of this conference was 'The Power of God'. It was not a difficult subject to speak on and as always God confirmed His word with signs following. Many people were prayed for and many were healed. At the end of one session a large number came forward for prayer and were overcome by the power of God. When I looked behind me it was a bit like a battleground as people fell to the ground overwhelmed by the power of God! As they got up many testified as to how the Lord had touched them or spoken to them through the power of His Holy Spirit. The board of Anchor Bay were delighted with the conference to the point that they told me that I was the first speaker that they had invited who actually kept to the theme! I have a plaque of appreciation amongst my 'souvenirs'.

I will not detail all my visits to the Philippines, but as I was planning my third visit, I heard from pastor Ludy that his village of Maigo had been overrun by the M I L F. He and his family had fled their home and had nowhere else to go but were sleeping on the beach. Thankfully, government forces repelled this attack and the village returned to normal. Ludy obtained permission from the Balangay Captain (I guess we would call him the mayor) for my visit to continue as planned. What he did not tell me was that in the house opposite his own house in Maigo were seven Marines posted for my personal security. I had known that on most of my open-air meetings that security forces were surrounding the place where we were meeting.

This visit was with a full programme as always. We travelled to new places and as was our practice we finished with an open-air meeting in whichever town or village we found ourselves. Every night many responded to the gospel of salvation and the healing line seemed to extend for ever but everyone was prayed for and there were many fabulous testimonies to God's healing power. The mountains of Mindanao are so beautiful! We travelled through these mountains visiting an army post that was part of the defence force against the M I L F. Many of the soldiers were Christians and we held a Bible study with them and many asked for prayer. One of my favourite anecdotes of visiting these mountain people was that in one village there was no hotel and no home available for me to sleep. As always, a solution was found and I was given a bed in the maternity hospital! My joke which follows is fairly obvious but I like to say it was the start of my deliverance ministry!

Pastor Ludy had a real heart for the tribal people. In one town, the elders from one of the mountain tribes came down the mountains to meet with us and with the Balangay Captain. The result of the meeting was that they agreed for Pastor Ludy to take his team into their tribal area with the gospel. This permission given by the elders was extremely important as these people have their own traditions. Far too often people will go into a tribal area without sensitivity. This naturally upsets the elders and more harm than good is the usual result. Sadly, pastor Ludy suffered a stroke soon after this. His recovery was slow but he was determined and it was not long before he was again up in the mountains working with these wonderful tribal people.

I really love the people of the Philippines. They are so very warm and friendly. When I have held open air meetings they respond willingly to the Gospel. As it is in sub Saharan Africa so it is here. They are so open and expectant that the Lord will heal them. Their simple faith has taught me so much. If the Lord has made a promise in His word, the Bible, then of course He will heal. No complicated theology: no trying to earn His favour. God has said it, they believe it and it happens.

Pastor Ludy died fairly recently. We thought that our relationship with the people of the Philippines would finish. However, his daughter, Pastor Eunice, has taken up the mantle and is doing wonderful work that would make her father extremely proud. Through Starfish Christian Trust we have been pleased to continue supporting the work that her father started. It is amazing how she has been able to make a small gift go so far. When we sent some support for villagers stranded because of the coronavirus lockdown recently, she reported back that she had spent a little of the money to hire a boat. At first we wondered why she would do this but it did not take us long to realise that she took many people fishing and was able to stretch the money much further. When you have little you find ways to become creative and are able to make a little go a much further.

I became a millionaire in Poland! I cannot remember how I was first invited to Poland but I spent a wonderful week in the forest with a group of young people for their Bible retreat. Their Pastor had a most unusual testimony. Living in the forest as he did, he would often climb one of the tall trees and sit smoking cannabis. His testimony was that he had an encounter with the Lord Jesus whilst up the tree and he came down converted! One of the most unconventional testimonies I have ever heard but God is no respecter of persons. But back to my riches! I naturally needed money for expenses, not least fuel for my trusty Lada. (What do you call a Lada at the top of a hill? A Miracle!) I changed £100 and to my amazement received well over a million zlotys. Unfortunately, I was a millionaire only for a day as it cost me more than a quarter of a million zlotys to fill the tank. Ah well!

One memorable church in Poland was a gypsy church. It was fantastic and as the speaker I was sat on the stage. As soon as the time to praise and worship started everyone on the stage picked up an accordion, a squeeze box or a violin. All I had was my hands. By the time I had clapped for about a half an hour my hands were raw but my spirit was soaring. It was true gypsy music – the only thing missing was a campfire! As the music played all the children started to dance in circles at the front. It was so uplifting.

If I was amazed to be a millionaire in Poland, I became a multi-billionaire in Zimbabwe. Inflation was running riot and even a 50 billion note was not enough to buy a loaf of bread! The invitation of Bishop Tshili was another that I had accepted through the Internet. I was not sure how secure it would be for a Westerner to travel through Harare at that time and settled on a flight to Johannesburg from where I took a bus to Bulawayo, the home base for my visit. What a journey! Having flown thirteen hours from London, I had just two hours rest before facing a sixteen-hour journey on a very African bus on very African roads with a very African driver. But we made it. On one occasion when travelling by matatu in Kenya, quite a dangerous thing to do, my travelling companion prayed that the road would be covered by the blood of Jesus. I had a picture of this in my mind as he prayed and I knew that my blood would never cover the roads in Kenya… or anywhere else. Once the Lord gives you a word it is good to hold onto it. On the many dangerous roads in the many dangerous vehicles in which I have travelled I have never feared. As I recounted in an earlier chapter, He gave me a word that not one of my bones would ever be broken and now I knew that my journeys were fully covered by Him.

I could recount many stories of the 'fun' that I have had on African roads. In the days when we carried big paper driving licences from the UK a policeman who stopped me could make no sense of my licence. He turned it this way and that and eventually let me go with the question, *"Geneva Convention?"* Of course I agreed with him and was laughing for several miles along the road. The funniest journey I think was travelling north to a small village simply called 'Gold'. It was a long way from home in the north-west of Kenya and earned its name from the mining. On the outward journey I was sat next to a man who was clearly and visibly drunk and in the aisle was a goat that was determined to eat whatever was in my trouser pocket! Once satisfied that he had collected all the fares the conductor climbed out of the open window and sat on the roof! The vehicle for the return journey was an open truck and I was sat opposite a very attractive young lady. She was sitting quite naturally bare breasted! It is better I make no comment at this point about the scenery! A complete contrast to when I was looking for a taxi back to the centre of Nairobi, having had a meeting in the slums. We found him in the local bar and he literally went over a roundabout!

I very much enjoyed the meetings in Zimbabwe. I will not give details as the accounts of too many meetings could become repetitive. Let me simply say that more than a thousand people received salvation and that time and again there were many wonderful healings. I will tell of just one. A young girl was brought to the meeting in a wheelbarrow as she was unable to walk. Let it be enough to say that she walked home pushing the barrow.!

Why do I concentrate on reporting about miracles of healing and stories of signs and wonders? I do not do it to boast or to report on what a wonderful man I am! If you remember Chapter One of this book you will know that I came from fairly ordinary beginnings. It is not about what I can do, more about what the Lord can do through me and therefore, if you trust and believe, through you. I have quoted already that God is the same yesterday, today and for ever. He never changes. What He did through Jesus in the accounts of the New Testament He will still do today. Jesus said to many people who He encountered, "Don't doubt, only believe!"

There are several words that have over the years crept into the language of Christians which are basically non-biblical. The first one usually comes when we are praying, and we use the expression, "Lord, if it is your will...!" I will concede that in certain circumstances we do not know the word of God and we seek him for wisdom, direction and answers to specific problems in our lives. However, let me give you a practical example which is used so many times. The Bible tells us that God is *Jehovah Rapha - the Lord who heals*. Psalms 103 tells us that God not only forgives all our sins but heals all our diseases. Isaiah chapter 53 tells us prophetically that Jesus, the servant King, carried our sicknesses, our infirmities, our lack of peace. These and other promises are part of the atonement that came when Jesus paid the price of our sin. 1 Peter 2 verse 24 tells us that by the stripes (wounds) of Jesus we have been healed. It seems to me fairly clear that it is the will of God to heal us. It is not His will that we should be sick or infirm. I will further concede that not everybody that we pray for is healed. Many times people ask me why so-and-so has not been healed and my only answer is, "*I do not know*". But that does not stop me from praying for the sick. It is God's will that everyone should be saved but not everybody is saved. But that does not stop me from preaching the gospel and seeking the lost.

150

Therefore, I consider it a statement without faith when we start our prayer for healing with the words, "*Lord, if it is your will...!*" I see a certain faithlessness in these words since we already know that it is His will to heal.

One other expression that has come into Christian language is, "*Lord, I claim this promise.*" Or "*Lord I claim that promise.*" God has already given us his firm promises and all His promises are yes and amen in Jesus. We do not have to claim His promises they are already ours. All we need do is to walk in them waiting for the Lord to fulfil them. It may not happen immediately, but if we wait expectantly He will do what He has promised. When I was about 10 years old I took the exam called 11+. My father promised me that if I passed it he would buy me an electric train set. I passed! I did not need to claim that train set from my father. He had promised me and I knew he would fulfil his promise! How much more will our heavenly Father fulfil His promises. No need to claim them!

I mentioned above that we do not necessarily know why everybody is not healed. But as I write, I am reminded of a time we were walking through a village called Sango on our way into Kitale town. Pastor John whose church we had visited a few days earlier saw us and accosted us and said there were many sick people in this village. Will you pray for them? Naturally, we could not refuse and went from house to house and must have prayed for more than 40 sick people. I am not saying that everybody was healed immediately and we went off to continue our business in town. On my next visit to Sango Pastor John again accosted me and reminded me of the day when we prayed for the sick. He told me that everyone that we had prayed for on that day had been healed. Hallelujah! If only we could make that our testimony daily. However, it does not stop me from continuing to pray and I do see many people healed.

There are many passages in the Bible that tell us that what Jesus did, we also can do. He even went as far as to say "*even greater things will we do than the things that He did".* Writing in his letters, the apostle Paul said that, *all the fullness of the Godhead dwelt bodily in Jesus, and we have been made complete in Him.* At the end of Mark's Gospel it is written that Jesus said to his disciples that as we preach the Word, He will work with us with signs following. There is no time limit on the promises of God. If we only believe we will see His powerful and miraculous working through us.

This is why I include stories of miracles and healing. I do so in the hope that it will encourage your faith. The same God works through every believer by the power of his Holy Spirit and every healing whether large or small should bring glory to God. If you have never prayed for the sick, let me encourage you to do so. I started small, you will remember, with a girl who had a headache. Start where your faith is and continue to abide in Him. Faith grows.

Sadly, whilst in Zimbabwe, Bishop Tshili's only son became seriously ill and eventually died. We were all praying for him but he did not survive. It seemed almost unfair that we were seeing many people healed and yet his own son did not receive healing. I have no answers. Only God knows the beginning from the end. It is good to include this moment in this book to demonstrate that we are not yet perfected in our lives, in our ministries or in our faith. I never see such moments as failures since everything is in the hands of God. They are learning opportunities and they teach us humility.

I cancelled the rest of our itinerary as it was obvious that I needed to minister to the Bishop and his family. They were naturally greatly burdened with grief but they showed tremendous strength in their trust of the Lord. There were two funeral services, one in Bulawayo where his ministry was based and the other in his home village. I had the privilege to be able to take the lead in both services. He needed time to mourn and express his grief and my taking responsibility for the services aided him in this process. He wanted to continue with the itinerary that we had planned but I firmly told him that at this time his place was with his family. I found a flight back to Johannesburg but my ticket back to London was not valid for another seven days.

Normally I would probably have found a hotel, or possibly gone on a safari, but I did not wish to remain in Johannesburg at that time as there were elections that week and my experience of elections in Africa was not positive. I searched the airport for a suitable flight but could find nothing until I found a business class flight with Air France costing £2600. A ridiculous price but better than being caught up in elections. I wonder whether this might have been my third flight home without payment, but on this occasion, I had a credit card. On my return home someone challenged me and said I thought you were living by faith. Why did you use your credit card? I challenged him of course. How do you think I will repay such a sum? Do you have the faith to give the money to me or shall I continue with my own faith? Needless to say, without letting this expense be widely known, I was able to repay it within about two weeks. What a faithful God. Let me say it again. "Only believe!"

People have been urging me for many years to write a book about my experiences. My response was always that it must wait until I retire. It is impossible to retire from the service of God, but I do feel that I have now retired from my travelling ministry. In those travelling years I have made countless wonderful friends. I am in touch with many of them. Over the years I have lost touch also with many and, as happens, many have died. I am often surprised when an email drops into my inbox or a message comes through on Facebook from someone who I may have forgotten over the years. I do not remember every name, every face or even every place that I have been to, but it is a joy to be reminded. I could recount stories of many more trips and stories from many more nations. - Japan, Australia, Cameroon, Honduras, America, Nigeria, and on. If I were to write about every country, every miracle, every meeting, it would be tiresome for you.

I have mentioned Starfish Christian Trust on several occasions in writing this book. This was set up to enable the work to continue even if I were to retire. It is still a very active registered charity in the UK. It is meeting the needs of many. Over the years it has probably seen more than £300,000 pass through its account. This may seem a small amount but it has helped many. It has sunk probably more than a dozen clean water wells in India. It has supported ministries, teachers and other charities. It has probably been instrumental in seeing more than 5000 people released from slavery. We have sponsored orphans and supported children's homes. We have helped in the building of churches. We have supported a work to take vulnerable girls off the street. The work continues. Any profits from the sale of this book will also go to support Starfish Christian Trust.

I have explained that we have taken our name from this story of The Boy and The Starfish and created what we call the Starfish Principle. We cannot change the whole world but we can change one life, one family or one community. Many of us see so much need around that we think that the problem is too big but even where we live we can make a difference one person at a time.

As I near the end of this account of my faith journey, I would like to mention two more countries. India and Pakistan. Both are special in their own way.

Chapter 16

Adventure in India

I have been on many unusual train journeys and I enjoy the different experiences, but none more so than a 'first class' night train from Chennai to Rajahmundry. Oh yes, I had a bed, but there was no real inducement to sleep. It was a bunk bed in the corridor of the train with just a curtain separating me from the hustle and bustle of people passing. My luggage was safe under the bed so long as I remained lying on it! Every time the train stopped, which was frequently, somebody came on board selling tea or curry or something I did not recognise. It was a long journey but at least I was lying down and at least I was not travelling third class! Having flown from London to Chennai and then boarding this train to Rajahmundry I thought I had reached the end of my journey. It was my first visit to India, having been invited through my website by Pastor Joshua. He was as excited about my visit, as was I. A quick meal at his home, spicy of course, and we set out to a town called Jangareddigudem. This was to be my base for most of my stay. India has such a large population that this 'town' was infinitely bigger than some of our cities.

On this first journey I fell in love with India. It is a country of many contradictions with a government working on space projects and yet with so many millions of people living in almost impossible poverty. I am told there are some 33 million gods and everywhere are shrines to some Hindu deity. Fascinating. My hotel was certainly comfortable but after three days of three curries per day I was grateful that my room was 'en suite'. I calculated that in my total visit I would eat some three dozen spicy meals. After several days I was able to reduce this number by having bread, jam and coffee for breakfast and mixed fruits with coffee for supper. All in all, it was probably quite a healthy diet, although probably too much coffee!

A large part of my early visits to India were to small rural churches. It was obvious that there was little or no income to build a church and to support a pastor but the joy of the people and the welcome that was always there was such a blessing. I had the privilege of cutting the tape to open a tiny and simply constructed building which was humbling. The congregation had given sacrificially for this building of which they were so obviously proud. I later heard that it had been destroyed by Hindu militants. There are difficulties for the Christian church with militant Hinduism. Even on my first journey I had a guard outside my hotel room. At the open-air crusade meetings in the forests and rural areas there were 'guards' to protect me. As always, in all of my travels in these difficult places, the Lord's promise of protection has always been with me.

The current president is a militant Hindu and also has many militant Hindus in his cabinet. I understand that his objective is to see the end of Christianity in India. Of course it will never succeed but he can make it exceedingly difficult for the church. It is now almost impossible to send money to a church or Christian ministry in India as any money coming from a foreign Christian ministry or charity is refused. At Starfish we have had to be quite creative to enable us to get money to India in support of the churches and the children's home.

As in many parts of the developing world, when a new church is started and a building erected the church does not have sufficient funds to buy the land. Consequently, more frequently than not, a local villager will give a portion of his land with permission to build a church building. This has worked fine for many years. Sadly, the current government, in wishing to register all churches, has decreed that a church must be able to prove that it owns the land upon which it is built. If it is unable to do this, then the building should be demolished. Pastor Joshua has recently reported that many of his churches are in danger of demolition because of this government action.

Pastor Joshua developed a great strategy for planting new churches in the villages. He told me that when he has about $1500 he has enough to plant a new church. He has a continuous training programme for this work. This sum of money is enough to cover the cost of a week of outreach in a new village area. After the seven days of outreach there should be enough new Christians to begin a congregation and from the money there will also be sufficient remaining to financially support the pastor for one year. In that year he is responsible for developing and growing the church and becoming self-sufficient. I believe more than a hundred and sixty churches have been planted by him in this way.

I was delighted to visit Hope Children's Home in Jangareddigudem. Having seen the conditions of the orphanages and children's homes around the world that have had such appalling conditions it was a joy to see how well cared for these children were. They have clean bottled water and receive a visit from the doctor every Saturday morning. Every child is at school and receiving a good education. I always enjoy a day with them and I am now known to them as '*daddy Stan*' (I prefer this to Grandpa Stan!) We have set up a sponsorship scheme and a good many of these children have regular sponsors which helps the running of the home.

Some of the children have been rescued from slavery by Starfish Christian Trust. I have heard some estimates that there are as many as 17 million people living in slavery in India. Sadly, because of poverty it is no rare thing for a mother with many children to sell one of them into slavery to enable her to care for her other children. The reaction of many people when I tell such stories is one of unbelief. How can a mother sell one of her children? As always the answer is never as clear-cut as it may seem on the surface. For the most part she is deceived by unscrupulous 'dealers' who assure her that the child will be looked after by their new 'owner'. In this belief she lets her child go and has, at least for the moment, sufficient to feed and care for her other children. All too often the children are abused, uncared for and treated as ''slaves' by their new owners.

I first came across slavery in the brick kilns of Pakistan (see next chapter). On one of my visits, Pastor Joshua told me of five children who were working in a factory and there was an opportunity to secure their release. I decided to see how we could help. The price was high - too high. I tried to meet with this so-called businessman but his secretary said he was out of town. When I got back to London I sent him a letter through Pastor Joshua and confronted him with the evil of what he was doing. As a Hindu he would naturally believe in many, many gods. I told him that he and his business were under a curse because he had offended the Living God before whom we must all stand and give an account, especially for how we have lived and treated our fellow human beings. I demanded the release of the children. I believe there are times when we should be bold. (Everything is HIMpossible if we believe!) He agreed to release them and they are now happily settled in Hope Children's Home.

This started a new aspect of ministry for Pastor Joshua and Hope Ministries. It was not long before he came to us with a request to release thirty children working in a tobacco factory. Again it was possible to obtain their release for about £20 each. The problem now was where would we be able to find care and accommodation for such a large number. Here was another opportunity to test the promises of God. It is said that when God calls he also provides. Once again He proved himself faithful to his word. Pastor Joshua was approached by a Christian friend who had just been able to build a new children's home which was being sponsored by a ministry in Australia. They had a brand-new children's home and we had thirty children. All thirty were given a home in The Light Children's Home and are fully sponsored by the ministry in Australia.

Since this success, we have been able to rescue several dozen more children from out of slavery. Some have been placed in the two children's homes and others were accepted into various hostels. Every child receives not just physical care but also pastoral support. How and when a rescue will take place is never the same. On one occasion Pastor Joshua had taken his vehicle for servicing and he saw young children being physically beaten. The work of changing tyres, not just on cars, but on tractors and lorries too was back breaking and they were cruelly treated if they failed in this work. He spoke to the boys who implored him to help. He bought them a meal and afterwards spoke to the owner who agreed to their release for a price which is the normal thing. We always try to negotiate downwards. Again, with donations received through the charity we were able to secure their release into the care of the Children's Homes. At first they needed hospitalisation as they were all diagnosed with bronchial problems. The doctor, knowing their story agreed to treat them freely. It is rare that the children being rescued are free from the need of medical care. In addition to the cost of release there are always medical bills and medicines to pay for. The doctor helps very much with this with but he himself has to pay to use certain medical facilities in the hospital. Through his kindness we generally only pay a fraction of the cost.

This aspect of the work for Starfish continues. Even as I write we are waiting for news of the rescue of another five children. Initially we were asked to rescue six but sadly one of them has died before we were able to effect a rescue. This is the sad reality of life in areas of such poverty.

There was a possibility that the Light Children's Home might have to close because the boys and the girls were sleeping in the same building. Although the girls were on the ground floor and the boys were on the top floor, as I understand it the authorities were not satisfied with this. We were asked if we could provide for the building of a separate dormitory for the boys together with separated ablution facilities for both boys and girls. The trustees agreed to commit to this even though our funds were low. The charity is also run on faith principals and this was one of the largest single requests that had been received. We were delighted that St Mildred's Church who helped us with the building of Sion Chapel in Burundi agreed to cover most of the cost of this. Not only will this satisfy the authorities but will also provide additional accommodation into which we may be able to put more of our rescued children.

Sometimes we are asked if we are simply adding to the problem of slavery by paying to release people from such slavery. We do not do it as just 'good works'. Every rescue is also an opportunity to bring people from spiritual slavery and introduce them to the saving power of Jesus Christ. If it were one of our own relatives I am sure we would do all that we could to gain their freedom. Jesus said that we would always have the poor with us. When we are able, should we not do all that we can to look after the vulnerable. It is the work of the kingdom of God.

Another question that we are often asked is this. If the children have been sold into slavery by their family what happens if the family want to take the child back into their home once they are free? If this were to happen then we would be powerless to stop it. I recently checked with Pastor Joshua who told me that this situation had only arisen on one occasion. When the father saw how well the child was being cared for, and at the request of the child, he agreed to allow the child to remain in the care of the children's home.

I have encountered some strange creatures on my travels. On one occasion in Africa I was bitten by a spider. I did not know it until I tried to twist my body that I realised it had paralysed me down one side. It took about eight weeks before this paralysis effect wore off. I cannot count the number of times when sleeping in the villages of Africa I have been attacked by bedbugs et cetera. I can remember going into a room with a grass roof and spraying before I went to bed. All the flying insects were soon dealt with, but I had not been in bed for long when cockroaches started raining down on me from the rafters. Yuck! On another occasion as we arrived at our destination at dusk we saw some scores of bats flying from the rafters of the home we were due to stay in. Needless to say, we found a lodging for that night.

In this context, I cannot remember in all my travels more than about five occasions when I have had any stomach problems with eating the local food. It would seem I have been given a cast iron stomach. One evening in India I was teaching pastors on one of my many Unity

Conferences when I suddenly felt more than an urge to run to the toilets. Without too much detail I can only describe it as 'vomiting from both ends'! This came as a great surprise to me as I had not been feeling unwell. The delegates insisted I return to the hotel and that someone else would continue to teach the pastors. At the hotel I felt absolutely fine with no discomfort and no repercussions whatsoever. A couple of hours or so later Pastor Joshua came to see how I was and had photographs of what was a large black scorpion about eight inches long whose name I cannot remember. It had been unnoticed on the floor immediately behind where I had been standing. They told me that this scorpion's sting was deadlier than the bite of a cobra. Pastor Joshua had never seen such a creature before although he had heard about them. If I had stepped back on to it my chances of survival were almost nil. I genuinely believe that it was the Lord who caused me to run from that spot. Yet another instant of the hand of the Lord protecting me.

Another difficulty that these poor rural people have is clean water. The yearly monsoon will often contaminate their water supply. Many die from the lack of clean water. When there is a new church planted often the Hindu majority will work to try and encourage new Christians to revert to their Hinduism. Not only are the church buildings sometimes demolished but the Christians are denied the use of the well in the village. They sometimes have to travel some distance for water which is usually unclean. We often receive a desperate call from Pastor Joshua telling us of the need of another Christian community that is in such a plight. I am not sure of the exact number but we have been able to drill many new boreholes and cap them properly so that the floods do not contaminate them. Even as I write we are waiting to fund the drilling of five more village wells. As part of the Christian witness we do not keep the wells for the exclusive use of the Christians but make them available to all the villagers. I believe in this way many lives have been saved from disease and death and I am told that this Christian witness has brought many to receive Jesus as their saviour.

As always, of all the opportunities for the kingdom of God which present themselves to me in India it is of course the open-air meetings. Pastor Joshua is one of the best administrators I have worked with and the organisation of these meetings is wonderful. He will arrange for small tuk-tuks (auto rickshaws) to bring people from the surrounding villages to a central point. The best time he says for meetings is in the evening and so lighting and carpeting on the floor et cetera are provided. I guess because they have so many gods people from India are incredibly open spiritually and I have seen hundreds of people respond to the call of the gospel. I always pray for the sick following the preaching. Again, these Indian people are very reserved and do not publicly express their responses. However, they are keenly open to recounting their stories to the pastors and I have received wonderful testimonies to healing. One evening there was a lady who was unable to get to the meeting and so we went to her home. They told me that there was nothing to be done for her and that she was dying. Having prayed for her we went home. The next evening she was at the meeting and came onto the platform to give testimony that Jesus had healed her. I have, in these pages recounted many miracles, signs and healings. As the people at these open-air meetings write in with their testimonies let me share a couple with you as they have been written. This first one is from a couple from a nearby village who came to the meeting.

We came to the meeting not knowing what to expect. We have probably been to some 1200 temples but we had never heard of Jesus. When we were invited, we gave our lives to Him. When the evangelist prayed for the sick we raised our hand to pray for our son who was not at the meeting. He has been mad (their words) *since birth and when we went home we expected him to be healed! We returned home, and he was in his right mind.*

As a result of this healing, all the villagers who knew their son were wanting to know what had happened. They told them that Jesus had healed him. As a result, many in that village believed and a new church was started. The church grew quickly but the village elder was not happy and told the pastor he must leave the village. Before he left the elder's wife suddenly became violently sick. The pastor asked if he could pray for her and she was instantly healed. As a result, the elder himself believed and made a building available that had previously been used as a paddy store. He cleaned it, painted it and put in electricity at his own expense. The seed that had been planted into the heart of that mother and father grew into a new church. When photos were sent to us later we realised that they had named it Starfish Church. We did not influence this decision - it was entirely from them.

Here is another testimony: -

I have given my life to Jesus after coming to this crusade. I am an assistant to a temple priest and have heart problems and my temple board could not help me for my treatment. I am very poor and do not have means of support for my treatment. I came to know about this crusade through the handbill saying prayers for sick. I came here wondering what I would get. I did not know. But I heard the simple and powerful message about Jesus and then started to believe in Jesus. Then you said you will pray for the people who are sick and I faithfully placed my hand over my heart. As you prayed God touched me. I saw the light of Jesus touching my heart. Now I feel like a young boy and very soon I will go for the tests but I am confident I am healed completely as I am not having the pains that I use to have every day. I told this to my temple priest and I quit my job. He asked me why I should do this and I told him Jesus had touched me and healed me. He is laughing at me. I do not care and bother. I will try to learn more and more about Jesus as I am able to read the bible.

Praise the Lord! One more…

My name itself includes my god's name. Shiva is an important god in Hinduism. I am fond of my religion and all the gods I believe. I used to visit many temples each year. When I came to know that a crusade is going on here I came to the meeting to break it up with my five friends. But seeing there were many people we sat down in the chairs in the last row and decided to break the meeting later. I am a heart patient and suddenly the pain started coming in the middle of the meeting and my friends are so upset with what has happened. I heard your good message about Jesus and did not even try to stop the meeting but was touched. When you prayed for people who are having sickness, and as I am having pain in the heart, I also put my hand and at that time I did not come forward. After you prayed the pain is gone. I am so surprised - I am speechless. I shared this with my wife and she took me next day to hospital and the doctors told me that I had had a mild stroke and I am lucky that I did not die. Jesus made me alive even though I wanted to stop the meeting. My friends and myself came to the meeting again on the second night and came forward with my wife and we accepted Jesus

It has been a real joy to be able to continue to support Pastor Joshua and Hope Ministries and through him The Light Children's Home. I trust that Starfish will enable the support of this and many other ministries to continue beyond my own lifetime.

Chapter 17

The Price is One Bullet!

How did I, together with a good Christian brother, find myself travelling into a Taliban stronghold that the security services do not enter even in the daytime? It was late at night and we were armed with an AK-47 rifle!

Pastor Moses was one of many who contacted me through my website. I felt prompted by the Holy Spirit to respond. (I have changed his name to protect his identity). His request touched my heart and it was not long before I found myself on a Pakistan Airways flight to Lahore International Airport. I had by this time travelled to and through probably more than 70 nations many of which are Islamic but this was my first venture into an Islamic Republic.

With the exception of the airport I was unable to get a bearing on the type of country it was. After a fairly rigorous passage through immigration we had a four-hour car journey to Faisalabad through the night. I was awoken quite early the next morning after just a few hours sleep by the "wailing" of the many minarets on the mosques which pervaded every community. For security reasons I cannot tell you the name of the Christian community in which Pastor Moses lived but I can tell you that when it comes to the sharing the Gospel he is a lion. Over the years I have met many good solid Christian men but I have never met a man whose passion for the Lord and for the Kingdom of God burns so deeply. He loves his people and has many times put his own life, and even the life of his family, at serious risk. As I looked out of the window that morning I could not help but notice three men armed with AK 47 rifles who were there simply to protect Pastor Moses and his family.

"You are most welcome to Pakistan, Brother Stan. I have arranged much work for you to do while you are here." Over breakfast he related how it was that he

needed such high visibility protection. He had grown up with Shahbaz Bhatti, the Government Minister for Minorities, going through school and university together. I had had the privilege of speaking and praying with Shabaz on the telephone before my visit. He was also the chairman of the All Pakistani Minorities Association of which Pastor Moses was the vice-chairman. (I also spoke at that time to Salman Taseer, the then Governor of Punjab assassinated by his bodyguard for supporting the loosening of the blasphemy laws and supporting Asia Bibi. See below).

Between my agreeing to go to Pakistan and my actual arrival, Shahbaz Bhatti, a good Christian man, was assassinated for his support of the minorities and particularly for the Christian minority. Pastor Moses was a nationally known Christian leader also. He determined that Christians would either go underground in fear or they should be called onto the streets in protest. Pastor Moses called Christians onto the streets to protest the assassination with big signs saying "Go Taliban! Go". This action earned him his first Islamic fatwa (a religious decision made by mufti) calling for his death. Over the years I knew him he received dozens of death threats. I later had the privilege of laying rose petals on the tomb of Shahbaz.

On that first morning we walked around the neighbourhood and I met several of the leaders of what was to become the Smyrna Church, even though the grand building that was to come was still only in the mind of Pastor Moses. (Smyrna in the book of Revelation is the city of the persecuted church) And of course everywhere we went we had a man armed with an AK-47 in front or behind us. It was good for me to meet some of the Pakistani people and for them also to see perhaps for the first time a Westerner in their community. I visited Faisalabad on five occasions and in all of those visits and with much travelling in the town and in the neighbourhood I have never seen another Western face. Whilst we read of many terrorist attacks in Pakistan, there has never been an attack in Faisalabad and I have since learned that this is a Taliban training city. In fact, there was a major Taliban centre less than a mile from the home of pastor Moses.

166

For very obvious reasons it is impossible to hold a Crusade meeting in any Islamic nation. The memory from history of the Crusades to Jerusalem are deep in the mind of Islamic memory. Whilst Muslims do not accept that Jesus Christ is the Son of God, they do accept that he was a prophet of God who performed many miracles and healings. They also acknowledge that the Prophet Mohammed did not perform such healings and miracles. For that reason, they will come to a Christian Healing Meeting. That first afternoon I watched as a huge tent was erected on the vacant ground adjacent to our home. This ground and the neighbouring plots would soon become the New Covenant Girls School that Starfish Christian Trust 'seeded'. This was to be the first of two nights of healing meetings to which all were invited. The tent was very elaborate and was fully carpeted inside enabling many people to be seated on the ground.

As always, I was extremely excited to be given the opportunity to preach the gospel in a place that I had not preached before. I was utterly amazed that so many people attended - there were more than 2000 people in attendance each night. In my 30 years on the road each new experience and each new place is opportunity to increase my faith. This was no exception. After many introductions in a language I could not understand, which was certainly no new experience, followed by a long period of praise and worship the time came for me to preach.

I have never been afraid to preach the gospel in unusual circumstances. Here before me were more than 2000 Muslim men and women coming to hear about the healer, Jesus. Naturally if I was preaching about Jesus the Healer I had to tell them who the healer is. It was with great boldness I spoke a message about the raising of Lazarus, comparing Lazarus coming out of the tomb with the empty tomb of Jesus. "*You can go to the tomb of Buddha,*" I boldly declared, "*You can go to the tomb of Mohammed. But can anyone tell me where is the tomb of Jesus Christ?*" I continued to tell them that if they followed Buddha they would follow him to the grave and if they followed Mohammed they would likewise follow him to the grave. Then I boldly declared but if you follow Jesus Christ you will not follow

Him to the grave, for as the angels declared at the empty tomb of Jesus, *"He is not here! He is risen!"* I believe that Pastor Moses slightly toned down my message as he interpreted for me, but what a joy to see some 400 people coming forward to give their lives to Jesus. Hallelujah!

Following this, as I have always done, I prayed for the sick. Having seen such a wonderful response to the appeal of the Gospel my faith was strong to see the power of the Lord to heal. Because this was a healing meeting many had come expectantly and many responded and many were healed. In many cultures, as in India, it is not acceptable to ask publicly who was healed but wait for testimonies to follow. Several imams telephoned Pastor Moses the next day with stories of those from their mosques who had been healed. The most amazing of all these miracles was a man who had been carried to the front by his friends. He was a paraplegic and as I prayed there seemed to be no signs of an instant healing and his friends carried him back. Thankfully, they stayed in faith and they did not leave with disappointment. They brought him forward in faith and expected him to be healed. The testimony came through the next day that he had been completely healed and we were told that he was so overjoyed he was even climbing trees!

Sadly, when people have the expectation that they will be healed instantly and this does not happen you can often see them leaving dejectedly. I always try to encourage people in these circumstances that the word of God says in Mark's Gospel chapter 16 that if a believer lays hands upon the sick then the sick will recover. I tell them not to leave saying, *"I have not been healed!"* But rather with the expectation and the words, *"I will recover!"* In this way many are healed as they journey home, some are healed overnight as they sleep and even for some the healing may be further delayed. Why is this so? I do not know. What I do know is that if we stand firm on the promise of God for healing, then healing will come. *"I have not been healed!"* is a faith statement. However, this is a negative faith statement that will produce its own fruit, i.e. no healing. Having said that, God is a gracious God and we cannot confine Him to such simple statements. He is in heaven and does just whatever He pleases!

The encouragement of these two meetings came with me as I visited several church homes where the believers would meet. I remember that Muslim neighbours had been invited to one of these meetings. Again, I was overjoyed to see people responding to the Gospel call. When it came time to pray for the sick, I was amazed that two ladies fully dressed in black Niqabs came forward for prayer. It was impossible to anoint them with oil as all that was visible was their eyes but to my surprise they allowed me to lay a hand on them to pray for their healing. My final meeting during this trip was to a funeral and once again I was privileged to be the speaker. In non-Western nations, the funeral is a great opportunity for preaching the gospel and once again the response of more than 50 people to the call for salvation was wonderful to see.

I never stop giving thanks to God for all healing whether great or small. All are miracles in themselves and I could probably fill several volumes with testimonies. Some are far more noteworthy. I was holding another 'Healing Meeting' on a subsequent visit at which there were in excess of 3000 people in attendance. As always testimonies came the following day. There was in that crowd a man who was visiting from Saudi Arabia and as I understand it he was smuggling Bibles into that country. He had an ingenious method of doing this but I regret I am not at liberty to divulge this as I do not wish there to be even a smallest chance that the authorities would be wise to his methods. At the end of the meeting I was praying for all who were sick. This man was not sick but stood for prayer for his wife in Saudi Arabia who was suffering from cancer. When he phoned her the following morning she recounted that at the time we were praying she was instantly healed of her cancer. Hallelujah! This reminded me of the story of the centurion who said to Jesus, *"Just say the word, and my servant shall be healed!"*

This first visit to Pakistan was a great opportunity to reach people that may not otherwise have been reachable and it was not long before I made a return trip to Faisalabad. On this trip too there were many meetings. There have been many times in my life when situations have become truly life changing. On my second trip I was taken to see the situation of Christian slaves toiling under the hot sun in the brick kilns. I have seen many situations of poverty and distress in my travels but the conditions under which these poor families were working all but broke my heart.

I have since learned a great deal about the conditions that Christians endure in the Islamic Republic of Pakistan. To a Muslim a Christian is a non-believer - an infidel - and they are certainly treated as second and maybe even third-rate citizens. They have very few employment or education opportunities. Many get into debt at the hands of a Muslim brick kiln owner and when they are unable to repay the debt the family is taken into bondage until the debt is repaid. Unfortunately, the debt is never repaid. The "wages" are so small that it becomes impossible for the debt to be repaid. I met one man who was not sure of his age but said he was around 70 years old and his children and his grandchildren together with himself had spent all their lives as slaves in the brick kilns because of the debt of his father. Imagine! Four generations labouring in such bondage because of the debt of an ancestor. Shameful! The Koran states very clearly that a Muslim is entitled to do one of three things in respect of a nonbeliever: he can tax him, enslave him or kill him. People ask me how I can know that the people in the brick kilns are Christian. The simple answer is that a Muslim will never enslave a fellow Muslim. It may be that many are nominal Christians but pastor Moses does have a network of pastors who visit as many of these kilns as possible. They do not only care for them but bring them Christian teaching and the Christian gospel. Some of the kiln owners even allow a small church service on a Friday, the Muslim 'holy day'.

When travelling to the kilns one morning, pastor Moses stopped the car, got out and signalled me to follow him. I was not sure where we were going or what was about to happen. There was a small crowd gathered around a boy of about eight years old. The story is that a few days before

170

the boy had been electrocuted and died. On that particular day the pastor was passing this spot and saw a huge commotion and much wailing. He went across and discovered that the boy had been dead for about four hours. He felt the power of the Holy Spirit surge through him and as he prayed for the boy, life returned to his body. Hallelujah! Although I have seen several people raised from their deathbed I have not yet seen someone raised from the dead. I have had the privilege of meeting several people with an accredited testimony of their resurrection.

At the time of this visit, Pastor Moses had been given some funds by friends in the USA and he wanted to use this money to rescue three slave families. The process was to establish the amount of debt which was then paid over to the slave owner. There are many pastors who work with the Christians in the brick kilns and with the help of these pastors the families to be rescued are selected. It must be difficult assessing those with the greatest need as they are all living in abject poverty. Once released they are given accommodation and the rent is paid for about four weeks. Employment is found, usually for the father if he is strong enough to work. This may be, for example, the purchase of a donkey and cart or the stocking of a small shop by which he may trade.

When I left Pakistan on this second visit there was a strong burden on my heart to do what I could to see families rescued from slavery. When I arrived home, I heard from Pastor Moses about two orphaned children in the kilns. Their names were Patrick and Maria and they were both under ten years of age. Other slaves were caring for them out of their meagre existence. I was able to find the funds through Starfish to be able to rescue these two dear ones but before I could send the money the news came back that they had contracted a disease to which they succumbed and died. This saddened me very much and once again I worked to raise funds so that on my next visit I would also be able to rescue families from the brick kilns. As I told the story of Patrick and Maria, many hearts were softened and I was able to take a substantial sum with me on my next visit.

What a joy it was to be able to see first five families rescued, housed and given the means of supporting themselves with the support of the local pastors. As we were leaving the brick kiln one young girl of about 11 years old by the name of Karishma approached me and with tears in her eyes begged me, *"Please rescue me. I cannot work."* She had seen the rescue of these other families and was desperate for her own family. We had rescued many other children by this time and I did not have the funds to secure rescue for her family but I promised her that, in the name of Jesus, I would send the money as soon as I was able. This was accomplished and on a subsequent visit to Faisalabad I was invited to her family home. It was evident that the rescue had been successful. The home was well equipped and all the children were attending school. It is these success stories that help to ease the pain of the distress and helplessness that I feel when visiting and remembering the desperate families in the brick kilns. Whilst it brings much joy to see these families rescued it also breaks my heart when I look back to see those that are left in the dust and heat, those for whom we have not been able to secure freedom.

Not every story ends with 'success'. One day we rescued a man named Joseph and his family. Life had been particularly hard for him. One day he had asked the kiln owner for help as he could not feed his family. His reward for this was that his leg was chopped of just above the knee as a discouragement to others to ask for such mercy. At the time of his rescue the joy for him and his family was delightful to see. Sadly, we heard a few months later that he had died. Thankfully, his family was still under the assistance of the local church. The local pastor agreed to continue with the work we had arranged for Joseph and to support his family in addition to his own. That is a great example of the Christian Gospel in action.

I mentioned above the assassination of Salman Taseer. He was assassinated for speaking in defence of Asia Bibi. One afternoon I had the privilege of meeting her husband and conducting an interview with him. It was enlightening to hear first-hand the conditions under which his wife was being held and the difficulties that he and his family endured as a result of her false accusation of blasphemy. This was also another opportunity for Starfish Christian Trust to give a financial gift to help the family. After much international pressure Asia is now free and no longer living in Pakistan

Because Pastor Moses had become such a high-profile figure in the nation of Pakistan it recently became necessary for him to leave the nation he loves so much. By the time he left we had been successful in seeing, in partnership with him, maybe 5000 people rescued from the bondage of that slavery. Not that we always paid the full price. In partnership with Pastor Moses we obtained the release of over 4800 slaves in one rescue because the owner had decided to abandon the kilns and return to his home in Bangladesh. The slaves had no income and no support, and we were able to persuade the local administration to release them into the hands of the pastor.

Many times nothing gets done because we say I do not have the resources. *"I cannot go to this place because I do not have the money!"* or *"I do not have the time!"* or *"It's impossible!* "Faith says that God has called me so I will start to plan because He will provide. We may be called to go as far as we can so that the Lord can show Himself faithful and provide what we do not have. Our faith does not rest on the fickle promises of men but on the sovereign Lord who created the heavens and the earth! It was a sacrificial donation from Starfish which initiated the release and we ran our funds to almost nothing. We planted a seed which secured the release of this great number but the need was much greater. We went as far as we could go. Our faithful God knew what would follow. A man from Texas arrived in Faisalabad and had more than $100,000 with which he wanted to release slaves. With this all 4800 were resettled, given their immediate needs and placed into the pastoral care of a local church. **Faith is the <u>substance</u> of things not seen.**

There is still very much more to be done. We can only keep applying the Starfish Principle of one life at a time.

It is a tragedy that Muslim men see Christian girls of almost any age as fair game for their sexual appetites. Many times, I have heard stories from the brick kilns of how pre-pubescent girls and young teenage girls have been sexually assaulted by their slave owners. It has been my privilege to see at least some of these girls and their families rescued from the shameful practices of the kiln owners. On one of our visits to the kilns we were faced with the dilemma of two beautiful teenage sisters. Their 'owner' was preparing to traffic them to the Middle East to work as sex slaves. Passport photos had been taken and their future looked very bleak indeed. We had no more money available to release more people but I promised them that funds would be found and they would be released before such a tragic event could happen. Next day I heard from a pastor friend in Louisville who had raised some funds for slave release. This was wired to us and with this we were able to secure their release. As we always tried to do, we found them accommodation and the father was set up in business. I can only count this a miracle from a compassionate and faithful God. The last I heard the older of the two girls had married a good Christian man.

I have seen a lot of war, famine and troubles but I was not prepared for the stories of two young girls - one was eight years old and the other was nine. I was disgusted by the way that these two girls had been brutally treated and sexually assaulted by older men. Young Rakhi was just eight years old. Because employment is so difficult for Christians in Pakistan many girls are sent to work as house-girls in the homes of rich Muslims. For some Christian families this is the only source of income.

The situation for poor young Rakhi is that one day she was alone in the house doing her work when she was attacked and raped by the owner of the house. He was an older man in his sixties. Following the attack she was in a terrible state physically and Pastor Moses was able to arrange for us to pay for her hospital expenses. As for the owner of the house, he was jailed but not for long. Corruption and bribery enabled him to pay his way out of jail and as far as is known he was never taken to court for this appalling crime. He continues to be free, but dear Rakhi has been suffering both mentally and emotionally ever since. Thankfully, the church has been working to help with her restoration.

Young Nirmal was only nine years old when she too was attacked by the old man who owned the house in which she was working. He also took advantage of her vulnerability and dragged her into a field where she too was defiled by him. Her story is similar to that of Rakhi but thankfully with the loving care of both her family and the church she has made a strong recovery. Once again the rich Muslim was able to bribe his way out of justice. I have questioned on more than one occasion how such despicable crimes can go unpunished and on more than one occasion I have been told that the Prophet Mohammed was betrothed and subsequently married a prepubescent girl, Aisha. I understand this is also why the government will not change the law to protect them. This together with the general attitude of Muslim men towards Christian girls leaves any Christian girl (or woman) susceptible to sexual assault and every Muslim defiler able to escape punishment.

I have already mentioned how Christians are persecuted in Muslim nations and not least in Pakistan. The blasphemy laws of Pakistan are often used by Muslims to persecute Christians. An accusation of blasphemy against a Christian is often met with mob violence. Such was the case in Joseph Colony in Lahore. A man was falsely accused of a crime against the Koran and it was not long before a violent mob had completely razed Joseph Colony to the ground. Most of the homes were destroyed and the Christians were left with virtually nothing. It was my privilege to be able to pray with the pastors of Joseph Colony and on behalf of Starfish Christian Trust give financial help to every family. It did not constitute a huge sum but gave early relief until other agencies were able to engage in rebuilding the colony. I was able to visit the Colony shortly after this attack as I returned to the airport and to my amazement the first building that had been re-built was the church. Such faith should be both a challenge and an encouragement to those of us living freely and without such persecution.

Another terrible example of such persecution was well documented in the world media. St Joseph's Church in Peshawar was attacked by two suicide bombers on a Sunday morning just as the Christians were leaving church. Such was the devastation that more than 260 men, women and children were martyred. I was asked by Pastor Moses if I would be willing to go to Peshawar and to minister to the bereaved and the survivors. As a Westerner this would probably count as one of the most dangerous places in the world to be. Before travelling to Pakistan, I kitted myself out with black Pakistani clothes and also purchased a false beard and a lotion to darken my skin. We struggled for many days about going to Peshawar and eventually decided the risk, not just to myself but also to Pastor Moses, was far too great to take. Had we been discovered, apart from the risk to my own life, the ministry of Pastor Moses would also have been seriously jeopardised. I was however privileged to be able to record a video message which Pastor Moses, travelling alone, was able to take to these suffering people.

Over the years I have heard many stories of how God is working to bring salvation in Muslim nations. For obvious security reasons these stories seldom become public. For example, I recently heard about a man in a Muslim nation who, led by the Holy Spirit, approached people in the street and simply ask them, *"Did you have a dream about a man dressed in white?"* Almost without exception he gets a positive response and subsequently is able to tell them that Jesus is the man in white and is able to lead them to salvation.

One incident in Pakistan which happened before my arrival on my final visit is a fantastic example of such a move of God. Pastor Moses was the speaker at a huge gathering of Muslims. As this was intended to be a multi-faith meeting he was asked to speak on behalf of Christians. Filled with the power of the Holy Spirit he boldly preached the gospel and prayed over the vast crowd. He subsequently received many calls, some testifying to healing and others, being of a more aggressive nature, making many death threats.

Two mornings later he received a phone call from his security people telling him that there were 34 Jihadis wanting to speak to him. He was initially quite alarmed and prayed with his wife. As they prayed they felt the Lord telling them that this meeting was of God. He welcomed them into his home and heard the following story.

"We are all Jihadis and we are here in Faisalabad to train. Our plan was to return to Afghanistan next month and make Jihad against the West. I was at the meeting at which you spoke and I came forward with the intention of shooting you but my gun would not fire. We are all staying at the same Mosque and last night we all had the same dream. Jesus appeared to us and told each one of us that what you had said at the meeting is true - that He is the Son of God; that He is the true way to God; that He died for our sins and that we can find salvation only in Him. We did not know what to do and so we have come to you."

On hearing this, Pastor Moses washed their feet and prayed for them to receive Jesus as their Saviour. He then prayed that they would be filled with the Holy Spirit and each of them began speaking in new tongues. They obviously could not return to the Mosque and so they were sent to various house churches where they are learning to grow in the Christian faith. I had the honour of meeting several of these men and hearing their wonderful testimonies.

Oh yes! As I asked at the start of this chapter; "How did I, together with a good Christian brother, find myself travelling into a Taliban stronghold in the dead of night armed with an AK-47 rifle?"

Late one Saturday evening we heard from one of the Pastors who visited the brick kilns that a family was in severe trouble. He said that their lives were probably going to be taken by the slave owner, probably by being thrown into the furnace. The family consisted of mother, father and six young girls. The mother had asked the owner for more food as her children were hungry. As a result, and to make an example of them to the other slave families in the brick kiln, the family were called together. The father was severely beaten together with the children. The mother

177

was dragged into a room, stripped and raped by two of the owners. The likelihood was that they would be murdered the next day by being thrown into the kiln.

The local pastor came to ask if we could pay their debts and rescue them. Apart from the natural anger that rose within me, I felt a prompting from the Holy Spirit that we should go and effect this rescue immediately. Although we took money with us, our prime aim was to rescue the family. I have been to many brick kilns to rescue families over the years and have often faced Taliban owners. On one occasion when rescuing families, the Taliban owner threatened, *"The cost of freedom for these families is one bullet!"* I did not receive the bullet, but the families were released.

The family to be rescued were enslaved in a brick kiln in the heart of a Taliban stronghold. Requests to the authorities for security cover were met with a more than negative response. *"You must be crazy! We do not go into that area even in the daytime."* For security reasons, whenever we travelled by car, we either had a security man in the rear armed with an AK-47 or else there was such a rifle inside the vehicle. On this occasion it was just Pastor Moses, myself and the rifle. We followed the brick kiln pastor on his motorbike as we drove in pitch darkness to the kiln. Fortunately, we had an element of surprise and Pastor Moses armed with his AK-47 pushed past the guard. They resisted at first but when he cocked the rifle their resistance stopped. It was easy to break into the room in which the family were being kept prisoner. We snatched the family and crammed them into the car and drove away at top speed before any alarm could be raised. The shocked family were sobbing bitterly in the back of the vehicle having only that today suffered such appalling abuse at the hands of the owners. Happily, the family are now living in a new city with the support of the local church. We were able to donate a donkey and cart to the family and they are slowly recovering from this horrendous ordeal.

Thankfully, what is happening in Muslim countries is not all bad news. The media stories of war and terrorism that filled our screens and newspapers are not all that is happening. I hear of many stories of how God is moving in great power and that all over the Muslim lands men women and children are finding true freedom through the salvation of Jesus Christ. I am so grateful to have had the opportunities to witness first-hand this power of God in Pakistan. Whilst it encourages me in my personal faith it does make me sad at the apparent weakness of so much of the church in the West.

Afterword

Onward and Upward

So there it is! I trust you have been blessed by reading this account and, hopefully, encouraged to seek more of the supernatural presence of the miracle working God.

However, the end of this book is not yet the end of my life! My life seems as full as ever since my 'retirement'. In my continued busyness people often say, *"I thought you had retired!"* Life is not that simple. I was recently contemplating this and came up with a sort of saying: -

Do not plan to retire – simply plan to change gear and your life will be fruitful!

Since I 'changed gear' I have had two significant and supernatural experiences that I wish to share. Recently, in a dream, I was with a large crowd of people in an upstairs apartment. Somebody told me that if I went out onto the balcony I would see God. In my excitement I rushed out onto the balcony and at first saw in the sky what looked like an immense plastic ring similar to those that people use to exercise. It started to glow with a brilliant white light but the light was not static. It was alive and moving in a way difficult to explain. It was moving in such a way that one could not see the movement and yet it was moving. As the Bible says that God is light I wonder if the light was moving at its own speed. As I continued to look the centre of the ring also filled with brilliant moving light but somehow in a different plane. I do not know how long I was all looking at this fantastic phenomenon but I woke with a start.

The Bible says that no man can see God and live but thankfully this was in a dream. However, when I awoke I was experiencing extremely strong palpitations which is something I have never experienced before. They were so severe that I eventually called for help and was taken to the Accident and Emergency department of our local hospital. Thankfully, they found no problems even to the point that I walked home in the middle of the night with no difficulty. As I have since reflected on this experience I believe that even though it was a dream my whole being, body soul and spirit was radically stirred.

The second supernatural experience came by way of a phone call one Saturday morning shortly after the above dream. A friend told me he had been praying and had a clear vision that concerned me. I cannot remember his exact words but in paraphrase he told me that he saw me and Jesus walking by the side of a river. As we were walking we were laughing and enjoying each other's company. By the side of the river flowers were growing but they were made up of light. From the trees birds, also made of light were flying towards us and flying back to other trees. As they flew, these 'light birds' diffused into many colours as they approached us. Each one caused us great happiness and laughter.

I am still not fully sure of the purpose of the first dream. Apart from the amazing privilege of seeing Him, I do know how my life changed from that moment. I seem to have a new clarity and understanding of the world around me and a new boldness in speaking for Him. Additionally, my interest in the 'world news' has waned significantly. I believe I have a clear focus based on a Kingdom of God worldview as opposed to a 'Kingdom of This World' worldview.

The vision that my friend brought took a little time before I started to understand. Since that dream I have found my interaction with other people has been more exciting. Without giving details, I have seen an increase in answers to prayer; several testimonies of people being healed and through supernatural words of knowledge I have seen many lives changed. With each of these encounters my dear Lord has told me that it was one of the 'light birds' that flew towards us and went off with the needed blessing to take to whoever was in need. That is why we were having such fun and laughing with happiness as we walked along the river. I believe that the 'light flowers' also have some significance. The Book of Revelation describes the trees planted by the River of Life as being *'for the healing of the nations'*. Although I did not pick any of the flowers I do believe they have a significance in bringing healing. I am still seeking more understanding in this.

I felt it good to share these two experiences in the light of my 'saying' above. My life of travelling certainly seems to have come to an end. In the last three years I have only made one significant visit to India. I have certainly not retired from ministry but have changed gear. At first I thought I had changed down a gear but life in the Kingdom of God works on a different economy and I have in fact changed up a gear. I have written the last chapter of this book at the encouragement and sometimes insistence of others. However, I believe that the final chapters of my life will not be recorded on paper. We are called to be a living testament to the love and power of the Kingdom of God and that is how I intend to write my final chapters.

My prayer for you, dear reader, is that as you have read this book that you will have been touched by one of the 'light birds'. God bless you!

Starfish Christian Trust

In the later chapters I refer quite often to Starfish Christian Trust. This is a charitable trust that has been set up for several years to oversee much of the work that is spoken of in these chapters and also bring a measure of accountability.

Starfish Christian Trust continues to work particularly in India, the Philippines, Kenya, DR Congo and Burundi. This is by no means exclusive as they will always have a listening ear for a worthwhile need that may be presented to them.

At the time of writing, the Trust is supporting two orphanages in India. We have just recently funded, with the help of a local church, the building of a boys' dormitory to increase the capacity of one of them. For the other, we have a simple sponsorship scheme which helps to finance the running costs. We are also continuing the work of releasing slaves, and this time predominantly children, and the two orphanages are a useful home into which many of them are placed. With increasing pressures on Christians in India, it has been our privilege to finance the drilling of many clean water wells in villages where the majority Hindu population denies them access to clean water. We understand this has physically saved many lives and bought many to a saving knowledge of Jesus Christ.

In Africa we are regularly supporting a CBO (Community Based Organisation) which is bringing hope to those who have no hope and seriously contemplate suicide or are suffering deeply from depression. Suicide rates in Kenya appear to be on the increase. Also in Kenya we are supporting a ministry that is taking vulnerable young girls from the streets of Webuye and helping them to turn around from a life of prostitution and addiction. They are being trained in skills that will enable them to become self-sufficient. We are supporting a ministry in one of the poorest countries in the world, namely Burundi. After much destruction in recent civil wars we enabled a solid and permanent church headquarters to be built for a ministry there.

There are two other ministries that receive regular support from us. One in DR Congo and the other in the Philippines. In difficult circumstances, especially as the world is changing rapidly, a little seems to go a very long way.

Once all the publication costs have been met for this book, all profits will go to Starfish Christian Trust to enable their ongoing commitments. If you would like to make an additional donation, or even consider a regular gift, you can find us at www.star-fish.org.uk. Alternatively, you will find us at 32 Mabel Polley House, Kempt Street, London SE18 4BU.

Finally, remember that nothing is impossible to the one who believes.

All things are HIMpossible.

Lightning Source UK Ltd.
Milton Keynes UK
UKHW020710251120
374025UK00005B/142